C000134731

Tragedy at
Tuskar Rock

Tragedy at Tuskar Rock

Mike Reynolds

With a Foreword by
David O'Beirne

Gill & Macmillan

Gill & Macmillan Ltd
Hume Avenue, Park West, Dublin 12
with associated companies throughout the world
www.gillmacmillan.ie
© *Mike Reynolds 2003*
© *Foreword, David O'Beirne 2003*
0 7171 3619 1
Index compiled by Gloria Greenwood
Print origination by Carole Lynch
Printed by ColourBooks Ltd, Dublin

This book is typeset in Palatino 12 on 14 pt.

The paper used in this book comes from the wood pulp of managed forests. For every tree felled, at least one tree is planted, thereby renewing natural resources.

All rights reserved.
No part of this publication may be copied, reproduced
or transmitted in any form or by any means,
without permission of the publishers.

A CIP catalogue record for this book is available
from the British Library.

1 3 5 4 2

DEDICATION

For the valiant cockpit crew, who fought disabling
vertigo in the dying minutes to radio the
only real clue we have —

'Five thousand feet, descending, spinning rapidly.'

Captain Bernard O'Beirne	1933–68
First Officer Paul Heffernan	1945–68

Let this be so,
His means of death, his obscure burial, —
No trophy, sword, nor hatchment o'er his bones
No noble rite nor formal ostentation, —
Cry to be heard as 'twere from heaven to earth,
That I must call't in question.
  Hamlet, *Act 4, Scene 5*

Contents

Foreword

When I was twenty-one months old my father was killed in a tragic air crash. Back then I was hardly able to string together a few words at a time. I had not reached that age when the answer to each question was countered by another *Why?* from me. Somehow I came to accept that if I asked about my daddy, or what had happened to him, the answer was not one I would like to hear. Unlike other children, I never became a *Why* toddler.

As I grew older and was introduced to more and more people, they would learn of my family connection with the Aer Lingus plane crash of 1968. Friends and strangers alike would offer answers to the questions I never asked. 'Wasn't that shot down by a British missile?' some would say with misplaced certainty. 'Didn't a secret British test plane crash into that, or something?' a few would ask. 'I heard there was a bomb on the plane' was another popular verdict to reach my ears. 'I was the son of the captain,' I would tell them, adding that I had read the official report from cover to cover. It only indicated that there *might* have been something else in the air at that time, I would assert. Following this revelation, there would be genuine and embarrassed expressions of sympathy from my listeners. A barrage of questions would then ensue. How old were you when it happened? Do you remember anything about your father? Is your mother still alive? I always made an honest attempt to respond, vowing that one day I would find some answers to the fate of the *St Phelim*.

In contrast with most of the extended families of the other sixty passengers and crew who died, I had been insulated from the immediate shock, numbness and pain because of my infancy. For them there had been no last farewells, and the healing process was slow, the flood of conspiracy theories only serving to keep the wounds open. Eventually the disaster became part of the modern folklore of Ireland.

My father's body was not among the fourteen recovered and other families and friends of crash victims were also forced to come to terms with the deaths, knowing there would never be a funeral to help bring some sort of closure to the grieving process. The inconclusive 1970 report, coupled to the many theories and allegations, left us frustrated and angry. Every fresh newspaper story or television programme simply added to our difficulties. This media activity kept alive the theories, among them, the missile conjecture. We desperately needed a new approach.

The 1970 report was the most exhaustive crash investigation ever undertaken by the Irish authorities. They did succeed in fitting together much of the jigsaw, but the important pieces were missing. The picture created by the 1970 findings did nothing more than satisfy the relevant official structures at that time, leaving the relatives in a state of ongoing puzzlement. And there sat the hazy unsolved case for thirty years.

Hopes were raised in 1999 when the Air Accident Investigation Unit began a review of the files in response to a lobby by the relatives. Some facts were highlighted in that review which were sufficiently disturbing to prompt the government into action. A new study was initiated in 2000, conducted by French and Australian air-crash investigation experts based near Paris.

Through the work of that team we have today the results of what I regard as an incredible investigative effort. Not only did Exp'Air dispel many persistent rumours and the missile theory, but it also filled in the blank spaces which had mystified us for more than three decades. It succeeded in offering a clearer picture of what really happened aboard Flight 712 on that fateful day. Its discoveries have brought a measure of peace to many relatives of the victims, and have stilled the restless minds of others. As for myself, and for my family, the conclusions of the study show clearly that not only did the crew do all that was possible to save the aircraft, but at times they strove for the impossible, and did that also. There is great solace for us in that knowledge.

Within the pages of this book Captain Mike Reynolds uses a lifetime of experience and a passionate interest in flight to tell the story in an accessible manner. As a contributor to the 2002 study, he guides us through the pathways which led to the startling and challenging conclusions. I am delighted that Mike dedicated the book to my father and his co-pilot, who emerge from the Study as the types of men I had always hoped they were — unlikely heroes aboard a seemingly ordinary flight on a March day in 1968.

David O'Beirne

Preface

O n Sunday morning, 24 March 1968 at 10:57 GMT, the crew of an Irish airliner reported by radio to Shannon Area air traffic control that they were cruising at 17,000 feet en route from Cork to London, and that they would reach the coast of Wales in a few minutes. One minute later, at 10.58, the pilot sent a distress call to London to say that he was descending out of control and spinning rapidly.

About sixty miles away, also at 10.58, the same aircraft was seen to be at low altitude, north of Waterford. Coincident with the distress signal, it was observed to be spinning to the right. The crew temporarily recovered control. Struggling eastward, they finally crashed into the sea near Tuskar Rock.

Aer Lingus Viscount EI-AOM could not be in two places at the same time. The reconstructed track, confirmed by forty-six witnesses, shows that Flight 712 was already in peril at about 10.42, ten minutes after takeoff. It sustained an initial upset while climbing through 9,000 feet, and never reached its assigned cruise altitude of 17,000 feet. So why did the crew report they had reached 17,000 feet, not once but twice? Did the pilots divert from the flight plan and lie, or did the certified transcripts of the radio signals contain errors of unknown origin?

Sixty-one people died aboard Flight 712.

This book is the story of the solution to the riddle and to the persistent theory of a missile strike. The astonishing answer was provided by a Franco-Australian international team of aviation experts, acting on behalf of the Irish government. I was a contributor to that 2002 study by Exp'Air SARL of Le Vesinet in France.

Acknowledgements

I wish to thank the following persons for their generosity and help:

The O'Beirne and Heffernan families, who made their photo albums available to give a face to the names, and who permitted me to reproduce cherished snapshots of the pilots who died. I am indebted also to David O'Beirne for his contribution of the Foreword.

My wife Pamela, who kept up an endless supply of tea, emptied the ashtray hourly, and who ensured that I ate occasionally during those long months when I lived in a parallel universe. Thanks for tolerating the faraway thought processes and the sometimes boorish glazed eyes.

Bernice, who used unashamed nepotism, so many years ago, to solicit priceless cockpit exposure for me on positioning flights of her employers' fleets, during her working stints with Skyways, Sabena, BKS, and Air France. The legendary aircraft included the Viscount, Airspeed Ambassador, DC-3, and the Bristol Britannia.

Martin Connolly, who helped me to recover a dozen wreckage sections in Wexford.

Lucy Tottenham, who corrected my syntax errors, and who adopted the role of a typical technophobe reader to suggest areas for simplification.

My four new children, who surrendered Internet time at the inexpensive off-peak hours, and steered their inept father through its labyrinthine pathways when he lost his way.

Richard Bury, who introduced me to the amazing literary agent Jonathan Williams.

Abbreviations
and Glossary

AAIB	Air Accident Investigation Board, UK
AAIU	Air Accident Investigation Unit, Ireland
AD	airworthiness directive to airlines concerning a facet of safety
angle-of-attack	angle between the wing chord or other reference axis and local undisturbed airflow direction
ATC	Air Traffic Control
ATCO	Air Traffic Control Officer
ATR	Avions Transports Régional, a French aircraft manufacturer
ATS	Air Traffic Services
attitude	relationship between the axes of the aircraft (longitudinal, lateral and vertical) and that of a fixed reference such as the earth's horizon
Bannow	imaginary reporting point above the sea, with allocated chart co-ordinates close to or atop lat. 51° 68′ N, long. 06° 12′ W
BEA	Bureau Enquêtes-Accidents, France; also British European Airways
Blue 10	air route with allocated and defined space
BOAC	British Overseas Airways Corporation
CAA	Civil Aviation Authority, UK

centre of gravity	point within an aircraft about which all the moments trying to rotate the aircraft are balanced
Certificate of Airworthiness	document issued by the State of Registry of the aircraft and applicable to an individual aircraft. This specifies compliance with the necessary airworthiness regulatory requirements for safe flight.
CVR	Cockpit Voice Recorder
damage tolerance	ability of a structure to continue to carry normal flight loads for a specified period in the presence of flaws, cracks and other damage
decompression	reduction in cabin air pressure to a level existing outside the aircraft. This may be caused by a catastrophic structural failure or a system malfunction or contained failure resulting in a safe descent.
DME	Distance Measuring Equipment
drag	aerodynamic force in a direction opposite to that of flight due to the resistance of the atmosphere through which the aircraft passes
empennage	tail unit of an aircraft consisting of a horizontal surface (tailplane or horizontal stabiliser) and a vertical surface (fin or vertical stabiliser) together with their associated control surfaces of elevators and rudder
ETA	Estimated Time of Arrival
FAA	Federal Aviation Authority, USA
fail-safe	design concept in which the crack or failure of any single structural element will not result in catastrophic failure of the whole aircraft structure

fatigue	weakness of material because of changes in the crystalline structure caused by the repeated application of stress
FDR	Flight Data Recorder
feathering	*see* propeller feathering
FIR	Flight Information Region (the start of the London FIR was defined by a boundary line on the navigation chart, approximately 12 miles off the Wexford coast)
FL	flight level (e.g. FL 170 = flight level 17,000 feet)
flight controls	controls governing the trajectory of the aircraft in flight, i.e. elevators on the tailplane to control pitch; ailerons on the wing to control roll; and rudder on the vertical fin to control yaw
flutter	aeroelastic self-excited vibration of which the external source of energy is the airstream
fuel control unit	governs engine fuel supply in accordance with pilot demand, ambient conditions and engine limitations
g force	gravitational force
GMT	Greenwich Mean Time
IAA	Irish Aviation Authority
IAC	Irish Air Corps
ICAO	International Civil Aviation Organization
IFR	Instrument Flight Rules
ILS	Instrument Landing System
lift	aerodynamic force acting perpendicular to the line of flight, caused by airflow over the aerofoil shape of the wing or tailplane
load	force exerted upon the structure due to aerodynamic or other pressures

mn	minute
NTSB	National Transportation Safety Board, USA
OPS	operations
PLN	plan; applies especially to the flight plan filed by the crew before takeoff
pressure bulkhead	structural item designed to serve as a boundary to the pressurised section of the fuselage
pressure cabin	portion of the fuselage of an aircraft which is sealed and pressurised in flight
pressurisation	form of climate control where an engine-driven air compressor increases the pressure of air inside the cabin of a high flying aircraft to a value which allows the occupants to breathe normally without supplementary oxygen
propeller feathering	where the propeller blades are rotated so that the leading and trailing edges are as near as possible parallel to the aircraft flight path. This minimises drag and engine rotation.
propeller pitch	angle between the chord of a propeller blade and a plane perpendicular to the axis of rotation
QDM	compass heading to be steered by a pilot to intercept a particular navigation beacon in conditions of no wind
QNH	barometric pressure in millibars/hectopascals
R/T	radio-telephony
RW	runway
safe life	design philosophy whereby primary structural elements subjected to fatigue damage are replaced at a specific time
SATCO	Senior Air Traffic Control Officer

Shannon	Shannon Area Control; eastern limit about 12 miles off Carnsore Point
spin	sustained spiral descent with an angle-of-attack beyond the stalling angle
stall	loss of lift caused by disruption and breakdown of airflow over the wing
stress	loading on structural material per unit area
Strumble	Strumble Head, north of St David's Head, Wales, an important reporting point. London Airways required an accurate ETA at Strumble to plan the approach of eastbound aircraft into the busy air space around Heathrow Airport.
SWG	Standard Wire Gauge, an obsolete measure of thickness. Millimetres now used.
tab	small, moveable control, hinged to the trailing edge of a primary flight control surface
tail load	aerodynamic force produced by the tailplane moving through the air. Tail loads normally act downwards (negative lift) in order to give the aircraft longitudinal stability.
thrust	aerodynamic force produced by a propeller or a turbojet engine as it forces a mass of air to the rear, behind the aircraft
VFR	Visual Flight Rules, with visible earth's horizon
VNE	Velocity Never Exceed, the maximum allowable design speed at which an aircraft may be flown safely
VOR	Very High Frequency Omni-directional Range. A radial navigation beacon.

| WWT | Wildfowl and Wetlands Trust, Slimbridge, Gloucestershire |
| Z | Zulu Time, which is Greenwich Mean Time |

Chronology
1968–2003

1968: At approximately 11.00 GMT on Sunday 24 March 1968, a Viscount 803 aircraft operated by Aer Lingus disappeared while cruising en route from Cork to London at 17,000 feet. The plane had taken off at 10.32 with a complement comprising four crew and fifty-seven passengers, all of whom died in the disaster. At 10.58 the pilot made a radio call which stated 'Five thousand feet, descending, spinning rapidly.'

Three months later the wreckage was located near Tuskar Rock lighthouse, about five miles off the coast of Wexford. A considerable amount of the wreck was recovered from the sea bed at a depth of 234 feet, but many important sections remain missing.

1970: The final report of the accident investigators was published in 1970. Some witness statements could be construed in a manner which suggested that another airborne object may have been in the vicinity at the time of the crash. A very strong rumour gained currency which intimated that an errant guided missile, perhaps fired from Wales, had contributed to the accident. That hypothesis persists in some quarters to this day, and it includes whispers of an alleged British suppression of the truth.

1999: In response to the continued allegations, hinting at a cover-up by vested interests, a review of the Irish and UK files relating to the accident was carried out by Kevin Humphreys, chief inspector at the Irish Air Accident Investigation Unit (AAIU), and his colleague and co-author, Graham Liddy. Their review led to a more realistic and balanced view of the missile conjecture, and revealed some serious errors in the Maintenance Operating Plan employed by Aer Lingus in 1968. In addition, some important maintenance records were found to be missing. There was also some concern that the man who had authorised the Certificate of Airworthiness for the aircraft, shortly before the crash, was also the man in charge of the 1970 accident inquiry.

2000: Because of the questions raised in the 1999 review, and the obvious conflict of interests, the Irish government agreed to initiate a fresh study to be based outside the island, and to be conducted by objective and impartial experts. Admiral Yves Lemercier and Captain Manuel Pech, both of Exp'Air SARL, which is based at Le Vesinet near Paris, were commissioned for the task, aided by Colin Torkington, an Australian and a Viscount specialist.

2002: The findings of the new study were published on 24 January 2002. It is the Franco-Australian investigation which is the subject of this book.

The Aircraft, Crew and Passenger List

THE AIRCRAFT

Type:	Vickers Viscount 803
Registration:	EI-AOM (named *St Phelim*, in accordance with fleet practice)
Flight No.:	Flight 712 (Cork–London)
History:	Built for KLM (Royal Dutch Airlines), delivered in 1957. Registered as PH-VIG, it had logged 16,586 flying hours by November 1966. Sold to Aer Lingus on 2 November 1966. On the crash date, the total hours had increased to 18,806.
Engines:	Four Rolls-Royce Dart turbo-props, type 510A (4 x 1,990 hp)
Wingspan:	93 feet 8 inches
Length:	85 feet 8 inches
Max. takeoff weight:	72,500 lb
Max. cruising speed:	357 mph
Accommodation:	Up to 5 crew, plus 65 passengers; the world's first turbine-powered aircraft to operate a passenger revenue service, heralding the demise of piston-engine airliners.
Range (max. load):	1,587 miles

THE COCKPIT CREW

Captain Bernard (Barney) O'Beirne. Aged thirty-five. Served in the Irish Air Corps (IAC) from 1953 to 1956. His total flying time was 6,683 hours, of which 1,679 were logged on Viscounts. He held an Airline Transport Pilots Licence and a Flight Navigators Licence. He is survived by his widow Bega, son David, and daughter Sally.

First Officer Paul K. Heffernan. Aged twenty-two. *Ab initio* flight training with Airwork Services at Perth, Scotland, in 1965. His total flying time was 1,139 hours, with 900 on Viscounts. Joined Aer Lingus in 1966. A week before the crash he was informed of his success in the examinations for the granting of a Senior Commercial Pilots Licence. He is survived by his siblings Des, Mary, Claire, Anne and Frank, and their extended families.

THE CABIN CREW

The fifty-seven passengers of diverse nationalities were attended by two airline stewardesses. They were Anne Kelly and Mary M. Coughlan.

Mary Coughlan had been flying for only one month on the crash date. On that day she had changed shifts with a colleague who had requested the day off work. The body of Anne Kelly was one of the fourteen recovered.

FLIGHT 712 — THE PASSENGER LIST

Archer, Katherine — Irish
Arnold, Dennis — British
Baeck, Roger — Belgian
Beck, Hans (Dr) — Swiss
Bryan, Elizabeth — Irish

Burke, Hannah — Irish
Cowhig, Michael — Irish
Cox-Ife, William — British
Creyelman, Jacques — Belgian
Dann, Sheila — Irish
Dann, Teresa — Irish
Delaney, Rory — Irish
Dreyfus, Pierre — Swiss
Dwane, Thomas — Irish
Faveurs, Edmund — Belgian
Gahlin, Karin — Irish
Gahlin, Sven — Irish
Gallivan, Eileen — Irish
Gallivan, Marion — Irish
Gallivan, Paula — Irish
Ganglehoff, Joseph — American
Ganglehoff, Mary — American
Hegarty, Edward (Fr) — Irish
Herlihy, Maura — Irish
Hinderer, Max (Dr) — Swiss
Jephson, Eileen — Irish
Jephson, Maurice (Brig.) — Irish
Jürgens, Theodor — Swiss
Long, Anthony — Irish
Meyer, Curt — Swiss
Mulcahy, Noel (Dr) — Irish
McCarthy, Christopher — Irish
McCarthy, Jeremiah — Irish
McCarthy, Rita — Irish
McCormick, Neil — Irish
Newey, Dorothy — Irish
Nunan, Richard — Irish
Nyhan, John — Irish
O'Brien, Edward — Irish
O'Callaghan, Bridget — Irish
O'Callaghan, Patrick — Irish

O'Halloran, James — Irish
O'Halloran, Josephine — Irish
O'Mahony, Nora — Irish
O'Rourke, Barney — Irish
Quinlan, Nellie — British
Schwartz, Paul — Belgian
Shorten, Ann — British
Shorten, Thomas — British
Sless, Ruth — Irish
Speleers, Albert — Belgian
Vastenavondt, Marcel — Belgian
Waeckerling, Madeleine — Swiss
Waeckerling, Roland (Dr) — Swiss
Walls, Desmond — Irish
Weiss, Rudolf (Dr) — Swiss
Zimmerman, Ernest — Swiss

Jeremiah McCarthy was an infant. Paula Gallivan was aged two. Marion Gallivan was sixteen.

Investigation Team, 2002

THE TRIUMVIRATE

Admiral Yves Lemercier
Captain Manuel Pech
Colin Torkington

YVES LEMERCIER

Born:
7 July 1933 in Brest

Education:
French Naval Academy 1956–59
French Air Force Academy 1960
Fleet Air Arm Pilot 1960–90

Experience:
During his naval career of thirty-five years, he held various appointments including aircraft captain, squadron leader and training operations safety manager. Logged 7,000 flying hours on fifteen aircraft types operated by the navy. Head of Air Operations in the Western Approach (Eastlant) 1987–9;

Maritime Patrol Aviation CO, 1989–91. Retired with the rank of Rear-Admiral.

Distinctions:
Officier du Mérite Aéronautique
Officier du Mérite Maritime
Officier de la Légion d'Honneur
Commandeur de l'Ordre National du Mérite

Civilian Air Crash Investigation experience:
Joined Bureau Enquêtes-Accidents (BEA), the French national air accident investigation bureau, in 1991.

Extended his knowledge of the new generation aircraft (Boeing, Airbus, ATR), and carried out many investigations in France and other countries, including:
   Convair CV640, crashed in Senegal
   Dornier D0228, Tahiti
   Airbus 320, Warsaw
   Airbus 320, Orly
   ATR-42, Morocco
   ATR-72, Chicago
   Airbus 310, Orly
   Airbus 310, Romania
   De Havilland Canada DHC8, Roissy
   Airbus 310, Nepal
   Airbus 300, Nagoya
   Airbus 330, Toulouse
   Gulfstream, Lyon
   Super Puma, Mexico (helicopter)
   Boeing 707, Istres
   Dassault DA20, Le Bourget
   Boeing 747, Tahiti
   Airbus 320, Mont St Odile
   Beech King Air, Bay of Quiberon
   Dornier DO328, Chambery
   Embraer 120, Clermont-Ferand

He was appointed principal officer in charge of managing accident and serious incident investigations in 1993, and was accredited representative to the NTSB on the ATR72 icing accident in Indiana (October 1994). Appointed in 2000 by the Irish government to lead the team conducting the study of the EI-AOM accident. Currently aeronautical associate expert within Exp'Air cabinet.

MANUEL PECH

Born:
7 October 1935 in Nice

Education:
French Navy Officer — Ecole Navale, 1954–7
Pilot Licence — French Naval Air Force, 1960
Engineer — Ecole Nationale Supérieure d'Aéronautique, 1966–8
Technical brevet in Upper Naval War College, 1969
Masters Degree in Economics (Montpellier University), 1969–71

Experience:
French Navy 1954–81: flight testing at the French Navy Test Centre (5 years); maritime patrol crew captain (6 years); project officer for development of the Breguet Atlantic turboprop maritime patrol aircraft (5 years); 3,500 flying hours as crew captain on ten types of aircraft operated in the French Navy. Retired with the rank of captain in 1981.

Aerospatiale — Helicopter Division (later Eurocopter), 1981–95.

Naval programmes director, 1981–7.

International deputy director of the NH 90 programme, 1987–95.

Currently aeronautical associate expert within the Exp'Air cabinet.

Appointed in 2000 by Irish government to the team for study of the EI-AOM accident.

COLIN TORKINGTON

Colin Torkington is the Australian nominee on the International Civil Aviation Organization (ICAO) Air Navigation Commission, the work of which encompasses the setting of standards on a wide range of issues from licensing, accident investigation, airworthiness and operations, to air traffic management. He is also alternate member for Australia on the ICAO council based in Montreal. He recently completed a five-year posting.

He was born in Yorkshire and started his career in 1952 with Vickers-Armstrong in the UK, where his final position was as senior stressman in the design office.

He obtained an M.Sc. degree in aeronautical engineering from Cranfield, and held a private pilot's licence and glider qualification.

Moving to Australia in 1961, he joined the Department of Civil Aviation as an airworthiness engineer, specialising in aircraft structures. He worked on several major accident investigations and as structures group leader in the investigation of two fatal Viscount accidents, both involving structural failure in flight. During his career, he undertook 70 overseas assessments and certification visits covering authorities, the manufacturers, and operators in 30 countries. He became head of airworthiness and operations in the Australian Civil Aviation Authority in Canberra; also chairman of the ICAO Continuing Airworthiness Panel. He is the author of 25 papers, 17 of which have been published.

In 1997 he was appointed to the United States National Academy of Sciences (National Research Council Committee on Aircraft Certification Safety Management), and he is a fellow of the Royal Aeronautical Society.

In 2000 he was seconded as part of the Exp'Air cabinet because of his extensive experience with Viscount crash investigations in Australia, and his experience as Vickers senior stressman.

1

Once more unto the Breach

A er Lingus Vickers Viscount EI-AOM, operating as Flight 712 from Cork to London, crashed into the sea near Tuskar Rock, off the coast of County Wexford. It was mid morning on Sunday 24 March 1968. The four crew and fifty-seven passengers all died.

The official report into the crash appeared in 1970. Its findings did not end the speculation as to the cause of the disaster. In particular, the rumour continued to circulate for years that a British missile or pilotless target drone had accidentally struck the Viscount and that London had covered up its embarrassment. Finally, in 1999, a review of the relevant Irish and UK files was conducted by the head of the Irish Air Accident Investigation Unit (AAIU). This review raised a number of disturbing questions, and the upshot was a decision by the Irish government to commission a new inquiry. To avoid any possible conflict of interest, the study was to be conducted by two leading French experts, assisted by an Australian who was an authority on Viscounts. The new team placed an advertisement in the *Irish Times*, seeking submissions from within Ireland.

When I replied to the advertisement on 4 October 2000, I was already an ancient mariner, an old retired sea captain with a lifelong interest in aviation and with a respectable number of flying hours logged in a variety of piston-engine aircraft. The crash of EI-AOM in 1968 had happened when I was based in Sydney and plying the waters of the southern hemisphere. It transpired that this was not a disadvantage, as my attitude to the disaster was therefore not coloured by the various rumours which had been circulating within Ireland for three decades. I could be impartial.

In my letter to Exp'Air SARL of Le Vesinet in France I did not mention my age. The organisation's notepaper describes its activities as 'Cabinet d'Expertise Aéronautique et Spatiale', and I had visualised the French Navy experts, who had been appointed by the Irish government to conduct the new investigation, as vibrant young scientific whiz kids.

When I eventually met the principals Admiral Yves Lemercier and Captain Manuel Pech, I was relieved to discover that both were in their mid to late sixties, retired from the navy, but still fit and sprightly. The Australian expert on Viscount aircraft, Colin Torkington, who was assisting with many technical aspects, was also in his mid-sixties. The team invited me to become their Ireland-based gofer and I was provided with an initial list of specified facets of the inquiry which required pursuit, especially the flocking patterns of local bird migrations.

There was only one real clue to the mystery of Flight 712 — the final distress call indicating that the aircraft was 'spinning rapidly'. I had experienced more than my fair share of spin recovery exercises during my early training days at the small Surrey airfield of Fairoaks. Trainee pilots today frequently learn to fly in aircraft which are not suitable for such aerobatics, and the instructor is often limited to a demonstration of an incipient spin, and a verbal description of how mishandling of controls can lead to a fully developed lethal state of auto-rotation.

The aircraft we used at Fairoaks was the legendary De Havilland 82A, better known to the world as the Tiger Moth biplane. I spun and recovered G-AOAC many times, high above an allocated practice area known as the Hog's Back, and using the spire of nearby Guildford Cathedral as a reference point to count the number of spin turns. I felt well prepared to show my best face to the experts. The Aer Lingus Viscount which had crashed in 1968 was a design from 1948; its tailplane was not a single moving unit trimmed by screwjacks, like modern craft, but had traditional hinged elevators and tabs which were controlled by simple cables. The Tiger Moth also has cables, I reminded myself. This Viscount was my sort of aeroplane.

On the pages that follow, I have tried to give an insight to the *modus operandi* employed in the investigation. There was no land crash site to examine, and no fresh clues among still-smoking debris. A Cockpit Voice Recorder (CVR) or a Flight Data Recorder (FDR) were not fitted to EI-AOM. These tools — the black boxes — are invaluable aids for modern investigators and many recent crashes would remain unsolved without them. (They are, in fact, coloured orange to aid recovery.) When there is a dearth of clues, a number of hypotheses are constructed to seek possible causes. Researchers can live with a theory for days and find themselves turning tiny shreds of evidence over in their minds for hours on end. Just when it appears that there may be some validity in a line of inquiry, a fresh fact will suddenly present itself to turn the entire original concept on its head. This process can often lead to an apparent schizoid content within a particular argument. In the search for truth within the discipline of an air accident study it is essential at half-time to change sides and defect to the opposing camp. A major criticism that can be levelled at the 1970 report is the fact that the authors chose to concentrate almost exclusively on the likelihood of a missile strike or collision with a pilotless target drone. 'Inescapable' was a word they used to support the presence of a second unidentified flying machine.

Within the world of aviation there was no high level of expectation about the outcome of the new international inquiry. Those who fully comprehended the technical nuances of this particular accident felt that the exact cause may never be pinpointed. The tailplanes, which are still missing, can probably provide the most crucial clue of all. What remains of EI-AOM in the area of the crash site rests at the edge of a shallow sandy depression, 234 feet below the surface, and close to the Tuskar Rock lighthouse. The most that was expected of Exp'Air was that some sense would be made of the reasons why so much emphasis had originally been placed on stray missiles and target drones. There was curiosity, too, about the absence from the 1970 report of any detailed analysis of the maintenance history of the plane. In the review published in 2000 by Kevin Humphreys and Graham Liddy of the AAIU, serious questions had been raised about many errors in the Aer Lingus Maintenance Operating Plan. These mistakes had remained undetected for a year before the disaster.

2

The Serial Killer

_____

U nlike my seafaring days, there was no navigation chart to guide my faltering steps in the year ahead. Based as I am near the foothills of the Wicklow Mountains, my cramped research office felt at first like a lonely outpost of the French Foreign Legion. It was a far remove from the sophisticated nerve centre at Le Vesinet, a mere stone's throw from Paris. There, at 36 Rue Alphonse Pallu, was based the collective wisdom and expertise of Exp'Air SARL, the cabinet of aviation experts now entrusted by the Irish government with the third inquiry into the crash of EI-AOM. Yet within a week I was to learn that the age of the personal computer, Internet access, fax machines, and direct dial telephones would shrink the distance between us.

Having laid out a large white cardboard sheet on my desk, I used a thick marker pen to construct a primary list of the known facts about Flight 712. It was important to have a clear and accurate picture of the incontrovertible flight path from takeoff to the final distress call, and to the fatal plunge into the Irish Sea. When the list was completed, I mounted the display on the wall, within easy sight of my desk. It was an aid I would glance at on many occasions during the coming months. In some ways it resembled the mnemonic board which often graces the detectives' room in those movies which concern the hunt for a serial killer. Or was the cause which downed the Viscount simply a one-off chain of cruel circumstances?

That very question prompted me to inject a series of tracer cues into a search engine on my PC, to check the worldwide total number of crashed Viscount aircraft down the years. The database at < aviation-safety.net > held some startling figures within it. Of the 445 Viscounts which were built, 143 hulls have been lost for a variety of reasons. About half of the losses involve fatalities, usually all on board — a total of 1,642 souls have died. Two of the fatal accidents involved Aer Lingus sister ships, EI-AOM and EI-AOF. The latter crashed during a training flight above County Meath on 22 June 1967. Three months after the loss of EI-AOF, another Aer Lingus Viscount was destroyed in a crash at Bristol. Happily there were no deaths. This was an 808 type, registered as EI-AKK.

The causes of most of the disasters are readily discernible, but some remain unexplained. Even allowing for the fact that the design owes its genesis to the industry standards which existed in 1948, and that it lacked the modern 'fail-safe' method of construction, which ensures that adjacent structures take up the imposed additional load if one part of the airframe suffers failure, a loss of almost one aircraft in every three is an appalling statistic. Although production ceased in 1963, repeated used sales caused this obsolete type to trickle down the marketplace chain to remote areas of the world, where adherence to strict maintenance schedules and intermittent airworthiness directives is difficult. As recently as 6 June 1997 a Viscount crashed in flames in Zaire, killing all on board. Many have been lost in Colombia, Indonesia and other distant regions.

On 24 June 2001 a Viscount operated by Transtel was written off in a crash at Ndjamena Airport in Chad, fortunately with no fatalities.

Having drawn up the basic list of known facts, it was now time to become familiar with the details of the final half-hour of Flight 712. The initial tools I put to use were the typed transcripts of the taped radio exchanges between the crew of EI-AOM and various ground stations. It seemed an obvious place to start. These certified documents detail the progress of the aircraft from the time it lifted off the Cork runway at 10.32 hours GMT until the interception of the last brief transmission from the Viscount. That final call came at 10.58 hours, and was recorded at London Airways Control Centre. There are also transcripts of radio signals to and from other aircraft during the first search and rescue attempts, and of the land line telephone connection between Shannon Area Control and London. A synchronous elapsed timescale, which runs down the side of each page, shows hours, minutes and seconds. These timing details are extracted from the running imprints on the tapes at the ground stations.

Old maritime habits die hard. The lack of some type of chart made me uneasy, so I decided to create one. On another blank poster card I drew a large map of the coastal profiles which delineate the land masses of south-east Ireland and Wales, separated by St George's Channel. I traced a dotted line to show the flight path from Cork Airport, passing close to Youghal where the crew had reported at 10.39 hours 45 seconds that they were passing through 7,500 feet, and were still climbing to their allocated cruise altitude of 17,000 feet. At 10.51 hours plus 48 seconds the crew announced that they had reached the top of the climb. 'Level at 170' was the call. At this point I changed the dotted line to a continuous one, denoting the remaining duration of the flight at its steady cruise altitude. When the first hint of distress came at 10.58 hours 2 seconds, it was possible to use the known cruising airspeed of a Viscount 803 to place a bold letter X on the estimated position of EI-AOM at that time. This location was then cross-checked by reference to the pilot's own estimate of his arrival time of 11.03 hours at Strumble Head, a promontory on the Welsh coast just north of St David's Head. At 10.57 hours plus 7 seconds he had transmitted a significant signal which clearly defined both his position and altitude: 'Seven one two by Bannow, level one seven zero, estimating Strumble at zero three.' The location described as 'Bannow' is not a real place, but a guideline reporting position above the sea surface, close to or atop ascribed co-ordinates of lat. 51°68' N and long. 06°12' W.

Thus it was that I began my odyssey, holding firm to the creed that a sudden and catastrophic upset had occurred during normal cruise flight at 17,000 feet, when the Viscount was but a short distance from the coast of Wales. Although I had no means to perceive it at the time, like others before me I was by now already seduced into a parallel world of delusion, one which had co-existed alongside reality for thirty-two years. The chameleon was hiding in the long grass, and he had changed his skin colour to green.

Yet all the clues were there from the very beginning.

3

Thin End of the Wedge

My first contribution of any merit was triggered by an incident of humdrum marital domesticity. It was only a tiny crack in the wall surrounding the mystery of Flight 712, but the small gap would later become a doorway. Like the death of Kennedy and the assault on the Twin Towers, I can recall exactly where I was and what I was doing.

It happened on a dark evening during the winter of 2000. Some of my children were gathered at the kitchen table, resentfully tackling their school homework tasks. Having expedited their duties, they scampered away to see the promised reward of *The Simpsons* on television. On the table lay a graph exercise book, and impulsively I jerked the blank twin centre page from its retaining staples. By this time I had become familiar with much of the 1970 report, but I had never seen a graph of the climb profile of the aircraft as it ascended from Runway 17 at Cork to its allocated cruise level more than three miles above the sea. I was not even sure that such a graph had ever been constructed.

When reading the disjointed content of any radio transcript, interjected as it is with irrelevant calls concerning numerous other aircraft, it is almost impossible to retain a minute-to-minute mental picture of the times of transmissions. Even more difficult to achieve is the ability to relate that timescale to the changing altitude of any particular aircraft within the distracting collection of signals from the other flights. The answer to this quandary is to draw a simple graph, based solely on one aeroplane's radio reports. This makes the progress of its climb path crystal clear.

With a ruler I drew a left-hand vertical line to carry the altitude scale and I added a horizontal line at the base to denote the elapsed time. The graph line started on zero feet at 10.32 hours, just as the aircraft rotated for takeoff from Cork. As each radio call came from a ground station, and each time EI-AOM reported her position and altitude, I carefully inserted a mark on the graph paper. It was by no means a professional job, but I was only looking for a rough guideline. As I joined the dots to form a visual story, it began to look as though I had made an error. The line did not have the appearance of a Viscount 803 climbing at a normal rate. I knew that such a four-engine turboprop transport, even when heavily laden, is capable of climbing at a rate of about 1,200 feet per minute or more. I checked the figures once again and began afresh.

There was something odd occurring each time at about 10.40 hours. The upward trend of the graph flattened out and the rate of climb fell dramatically below normal. Between 10.36 and 10.40 hours it was below 400 feet per minute. I was hampered by a lack of specialist knowledge of the operational procedures used by Viscount crews in 1968 on the Cork to London service. Common sense told me it was most unlikely that any noise abatement requirements existed for the relatively quiet turboprop, particularly at 6,000 feet above open country. A brief 'step' may occur during transition from high takeoff power to the reduced climb power setting,

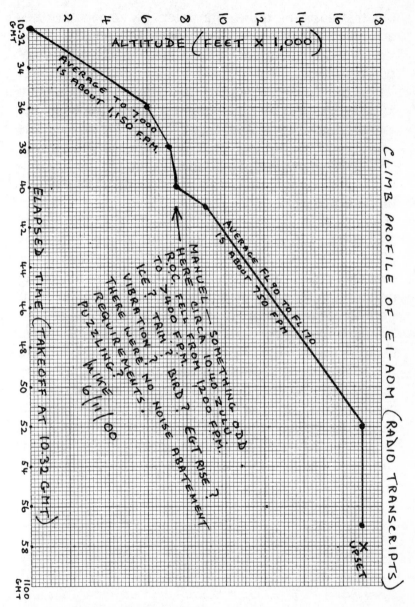

Draft graph of the climb profile of EI-AOM prepared by the author and sent by him to Exp'Air in November 2000.

but this happens quite soon after the wheels and any takeoff flap are retracted, and after a safe positive climb rate is established, with all engines delivering normal power.

As the climb rate started to increase again, I sought to determine the average figure up to the time when the aircraft reached its stated cruise level of 17,000 feet. The average climb rate to 17,000 feet from takeoff showed only 850 feet per minute. Reductions due to density altitude variation will progressively slow the rate of climb, but it is not until 15,000 feet is reached that a Viscount slows to half the sea level figure. From 9,000 feet to 17,000 feet, the average rate of climb was a little over 750 feet per minute. Either it was time for me to do a refresher course in basic maths, or there was something ominous in the figures which I had not spotted from perusal of the lines of text.

On 6 November 2000 I wrote to the French team, enclosing my crude offering of the graph (the complete memorandum is reproduced in Appendix 2C). I drew the attention of Exp'Air to the strange anomaly in the climb performance of Flight 712. If a mistake existed in my figures for the graph presentation, or if I had overlooked some hidden factor or simple explanation, the experts would quickly spot my miscalculation and point it out to me.

There was no error.

4

Collision Course

Inow had a possible starting point, which was the pronounced blip on the graph of the aircraft's climb path. Something had caused it and I made a list of the usual suspects. Ice accretion? Trim problem? Bird strike? A sticky control cable run? Temporary vibration? A rise in exhaust gas temperature on an engine? Whatever occurred, it seemed that it was relatively innocuous at the time and transitory. It had not been of sufficient importance to warrant a radio call to inform Shannon. The subsequent routine transmissions from EI-AOM were delivered in normal laconic tones, with no hint of anxiety on the flight deck.

I began by examining the remote possibility of a glancing bird strike which might have inflicted only limited skin damage at first, with progressive deterioration of the affected airfoil. The initiation of the graph aberration was centred at an altitude below 10,000 feet. A little over five years earlier another Viscount had crashed when a Whistling swan struck the tail at 6,000 feet, killing all on board. The United Airlines flight, en route between Newark and Washington on 23 November 1962, encountered the flock above Ellicott City in Maryland. The left tailplane was severed from the fuselage when it took a direct hit.

My limited flying hours have nurtured within me a great admiration for the aviation exploits of migrating birds and their long, often incredible, journeys. Though I am not an expert on these flights, my lifelong interest had generated sufficient knowledge to prompt me to question the accuracy of those conclusions in the original 1970 report which related to the possibility of a bird strike. The findings looked sloppy, incomplete and inaccurate. It was almost as though the authors were so distracted by their focus on errant guided missiles fired from Wales that they lacked the conviction and zeal required to seriously consider all or any other possibilities.

The 1970 investigation had examined the possibility of a strike by Greenland white-fronted geese. However, since these birds head north on their departure track from the Wexford sloblands, their course would have taken them well clear of the route flown by EI-AOM. It seemed strange to me that the report had concentrated almost exclusively on this species, ignoring Bewick's swans and other, more likely, contenders on the list of collision suspects. I spent some weeks of intense study of all available data on any birds whose movements could put them on potential collision courses with EI-AOM. It was relatively easy to formulate a hypothesis for a strike during the climb phase between Cork and the Wexford coast, an area replete with wetland sites. But now I also turned my attention to the possibilities of collision with a bird at the cruise level of 17,000 feet, where the sudden upset had apparently occurred. It was important to discover if Irish flocks ever traversed the skies at that height.

Within days I had established some interesting facts. The all-time altitude record for birds which spend winter in Ireland is held by a flock of Whooper swans from Iceland, spotted above the Outer Hebrides as they descended towards Ireland for the winter feeding regime. The birds were flying at 26,400 feet, some five miles above sea level. I also discovered that flocks of Bewick's swans leave Ireland for Siberia and other breeding locations in March, crossing the Irish Sea and St George's Channel in the process. I wrote to Exp'Air, questioning the conclusion in the 1970 report which had stated that the evidence of a possible bird strike was 'negative' (the complete memorandum is reproduced in Appendix 2D). The astonishing altitude record for Whooper swans had been filed as an air-miss report by a flight crew. It was a known incident, and well documented in aviation circles at the time the 1970 report was prepared. I could not understand why the authors had dismissed it all so lightly. I was now eyeing the original report contents in greater detail and with caution. Moreover, the hairs on the back of my neck stood up when I first saw the eerie date of that swan altitude record, which still stands today. The birds had been tracked all the way by radar on 9 December 1967, with some flocks touching down as far south as Kerry and at Kilcolman in County Cork. They were the very same flocks which would depart in a few months on the annual return to their distant breeding grounds. These altitude record-holders would take off from Ireland during March 1968, the month of the crash.

5

The Climb

For weeks on end the birds kept intruding on my thoughts. I found it impossible to explain the climb aberrations within the tape transcript of the time period which immediately followed the control changeover from Cork to Shannon at about 10.40 hours. If the graph irregularity, with its abnormal climb rate, was induced by any serious problem arising from control difficulties or power loss, it was utterly inconceivable that the crew would have continued the flight to the cruise level of 17,000 feet. At the very least, they would have informed Shannon of their predicament by radio and opted to return to Cork for a precautionary landing. The very fact that they continued the flight without comment indicated that there had been no engine problem or impairment of control arising from failure of any part of the airframe, or of the tail surfaces. This ruled out the likelihood of fatigue cracks or corrosion as a factor, since they usually result in immediate and devastating effects. The strange characteristics of the average rate of climb exhibited by EI-AOM continued to pose a mystery.

As I wrestled with every imaginable scenario, the nucleus of an idea emerged which could fit into the equation. I decided to include it in support of my bird-strike proposal to Exp'Air. In essence, I suggested that Flight 712 might have encountered her initial problem quite early in the climb, and not as a sudden occurrence at cruise altitude near the coast of Wales. In November 2000 I tied all the threads together in a memo to France:

RE: A BIRD-STRIKE HYPOTHESIS (CLIMB PHASE)
Suppose EI-AOM struck a low-altitude swan or goose from the Cork wetlands during the initial climb-out, say between 500 and 2,000 feet. This could have inflicted only minor damage to the leading edge of a tailplane. There is often a little turbulence during the initial climb, which on the day of the crash was through a cloud base at 2,000 feet with the tops at 6,000 feet. Any mild buffeting from slight tailplane damage, if it existed, would not necessarily alarm the crew. Minor damage to the tail might cause temporary vibration in the control column, which could disappear again with a modest elevator trim tab alteration, restoring deceptive confidence after a 'feel-out' of the control runs by the crew. The climb angle of a Viscount was probably not as high as on modern jets, but it could still possibly have restricted the forward vision of the crew, who may not have spotted a flock, or an individual bird. When the aircraft was trimmed at the top of the climb, during transition to the cruise altitude of 17,000 feet, there would have been an increase in airspeed and an alteration in the angle-of-attack of the tailplanes.

Suppose these changes in angle and relative airflow started to exacerbate any initial minor tear, opening the tail skin fully, or causing a spar or web plate to fail? Enclosed is a comparative summary report on Embraer Brasilia N33701, which entered a fatal spin similar to EI-AOM during transition from cruise to descent. Like the climb strike hypothesis just mentioned, the ill-fitted left tailplane on the Brasilia did its job at the aerodynamic loads imposed during climb and cruise. It was not until there was a *change* in that load as the descent started, and with altered tailplane angle-of-attack, that the leading edge failed abruptly on the left side. EI-AOM, which had been cleared direct to Strumble Head, had not long established cruise flight when the crew called 'Echo India Alpha Oscar Mike ... with you', an uncommon, curious text of transmission which hints at incipient anxiety on the flight deck. When we next heard from EI-AOM, eight seconds later, it was spinning down through 5,000 feet.

There were 47 critical screws missing from the left tailplane leading edge assembly on the Brasilia N33701, owing to an error in a changeover of a workers' shift. Do any of the missing maintenance records at Aer Lingus relate to tailplanes? Did the undetected errors in their Maintenance Operating Plan, existing for a full year before the disaster, have any connection with the tail areas?

The scenario I had painted concerning a possible cancellation of control column vibration by use of elevator trim experimentation prompted me to recall an accident in the US which was caused by distraction of the crew. The aircraft was in descent when the pilots became obsessed by a faulty warning light in an instrument. Their heads were down in the cockpit as they fiddled with the fault for a long period. They failed to notice their rate of descent and the aircraft impacted a swamp, killing all aboard. Perhaps an attempt could have been made by the crew of EI-AOM to reduce or eliminate any tail vibration with gradual 'stepped' power reductions. If the climb speed fell dangerously low, there always existed a possibility that a stall could ensue, causing a dive and recovery.

My ruminations were not very encouraging. All I had was a very crude graph with an odd-looking flat spot and the hint of a climb rate which resembled in part the performance of an under-powered Piper Cub. Added to this was a half-baked proposition that the Viscount could have been in some type of trouble a lot earlier than had been believed. At best they were two unsteady props, not suited as legs to support the beginnings of a credible thesis. I badly needed an extra leg to make a more stable tripod. It was to come in the form of a tiny length of tungsten wire, shorter than the width of a fingernail and slightly thicker than a human hair.

6

Mute Witness

Sometimes the building blocks which assist a hypothesis are not of the large nine-inch cavity variety. They can be as small as a piece of Lego, but when they slot into place they make the same reassuring, positive click as that childhood construction toy.

When a domestic light bulb fails, often just as the light switch clicks on, we discard the defunct globe and insert a new one. But if you are lucky enough to discover a small burned-out electric bulb amid the mass of wreckage from a crashed aircraft, it's as though you have stumbled on a gold nugget. It is immediately packed in cotton wool within a suitable container, and despatched to a laboratory for close scrutiny. It may well have a story to tell.

Within the appendices of the 1970 report are a few brief words about just such a routine examination. As I pondered on it for a day or two I began to believe that insufficient attention had been paid to the lab technician's finding. In fact, it had been practically ignored apart from some inconclusive comments. A bulb from a Fasten Seat Belt/No Smoking sign aboard EI-AOM had been examined and it had delivered a small pointer. It was a tiny clue, but now it began to assume some significance when viewed in conjunction with the apparent conundrum within the graph of the climb.

Let me take you into the strange world of the men and women who spend their working days peering at tiny slivers through the eyepiece of a powerful microscope. The bulb from Flight 712 is placed within a vice with soft protected jaws and at minimum pressure. A tiny sharp bit on an electric drill chews its way through the bayonet fitting, slowing its revolutions as it nears the inside surface. It stays in place while the tip breaks through, acting as a blockage in the drilled hole to dampen the inlet hiss of atmospheric pressure. Air fills the vacuum within the glass. Brittle adhesive which connects the brass cap to the globe is chipped away, and with a final firm twist the cap separates. Rolling around within the inverted glass, and just visible to the naked eye, are the priceless pieces of the hair-like coils which originally formed the filament of ductile tungsten wire. The technician gently cracks the glass open and eases the recovered wire sections on to the examination slide.

When EI-AOM struck the sea surface at a high rate of vertical descent, and with a forward airspeed component below 130 knots, the impact load on the bulb filament caused it to snap. If the sign was switched on during the split second that followed, the voltage potential would continue until the catastrophic break-up of the fuselage destroyed the supply cables. If the sign was off, the cold ends of the broken filament should show a clean break, with rough cross-section surfaces.

At a modest magnification of x20 the symmetric rounded beads of melted tungsten at the ends of the break are visible. As the filament snapped, the flow of current jumped for a millisecond across the initial opening gap between the two severed ends, creating an electric arc and the tell-tale globules. Power up the magnification to x40 and now you can see where the cantilever forces, exerted at the small metal posts which supported the filament, caused the broken coiled wire to stretch and wave about. This threshing motion led to further contacts between the dying glowing filament and other parts of the bulb. Those smaller balls of tungsten, which can now be seen, result from the dissipation of that energy. We know this, because the balls are asymmetric in shape, unlike the initial arc gap with its perfectly rounded ends. To complete the picture, there are even a few fused particles of glass to be seen. There is now no further doubt. The Fasten Seat Belt/No Smoking signs were illuminated when the crash occurred.

It was time to add some extra impetus to the argument which favoured an early incident of unknown origin during the climb above south-east Ireland. Weather conditions at the time excluded any likelihood of uncomfortable turbulence at the cruise level. If EI-AOM had experienced a sudden fatal spin at 17,000 feet with no advance warning, or had encountered a missile, the instant struggle in the cockpit to regain control would create a plight for the crew wherein mundane actions, like switching on the seat belt signs, would be the last thing on their minds.

I shared my puzzlement with Yves and Manuel in November 2000:

> It was fairly common to switch off the cabin signs after the climb was comfortably established and turbulence was absent. EI-AOM had just reached cruise level, when the sudden upset occurred some minutes later.
>
> I thought it curious that the 1970 report (Sec.2.1.4.6) said there was evidence that the signs were 'on'. A recovered bulb filament had failed 'hot' under crash impact load. There was also medical evidence that some seat belts were fastened. The report did not

examine these matters any further. The abrupt spin which occurred would not prompt the startled crew to start thinking about cabin signs, a routine reserved for normal operations.

So, if the signs and belts were 'on', why?

Whatever had happened to Flight 712 to bring about its destruction, there was now a glimmer of evidence from more than one source that it may not have been as sudden and immediately calamitous as had always been assumed. At some stage after the initial upset a modicum of partial control must have been achieved, which gave the crew a brief opportunity to instruct the passengers to fasten seat belts and extinguish cigarettes. The problem with that hypothesis was that any such breathing space also gave the crew a chance to send a brief radio message.

So why were the airwaves silent?

7

The Beachcomber

The promontory of Greenore Point juts out into St George's Channel. From this headland, a beach runs north-west to the ferry port of Rosslare. It is the closest part of the mainland to the Tuskar Rock lighthouse, which is about five miles offshore. In a neat home near by lives Martin Connolly. When I first heard of Martin he had no name, just a number. Witness No. 17, to be exact.

Martin, who had seen the column of water displaced by the aircraft as it hit the sea, was a beachcomber. In October 1968 he had found a small but significant piece of wreckage on the beach near his home. In his statement to the 1970 investigators he had indicated that the item was enfolded in seaweed. There are many varieties of these marine growths, all of various shapes and colours. It would be a very long shot after three decades, but if the beachcomber could recall the exact colour of the weed, it might help to pinpoint the original location and depth where the piece had initially fallen and lain. I enlisted the aid of Professor Mike Guiry of University College Galway, who is a leading seaweed specialist. He suggested that I should also consider that the section could have fallen on one of the thousands of large floating rafts of weed, anywhere below the flight path, and then drifted to the shore. I wondered if Martin was still alive, or living in the area.

The police at Rosslare pier successfully traced him, and Garda Tom Kennedy gave me Martin's phone number. He has built a new home about two hundred yards from his now derelict thatched abode of 1968, but still overlooking the sea and the Tuskar Rock lighthouse. The phone call started with the usual polite civilities. Yes, he said, he remembered the brown seaweed quite well. It was a dark shade of brown. Definitely not green. Nor red. Not yellow, either. We chatted about the disaster in general terms for a while and eventually I felt that there was not much more to discuss. As a parting word, I casually enquired about the dimensions of the wreckage item he had found in 1968. His answer set my heart pounding: 'Not very big, really. It was about the same size as some of those other pieces which we kept as souvenirs of the crash.'

For a moment or two I stood in stunned silence. In fairness to Martin he had no real appreciation of the implications of what he had just said. Air-crash investigation techniques are a world apart from a man whose life-style is so uncomplicated, searching for anything of value which the sea surrenders. I asked him if the pieces had been in the sea for a long time. No, they were recovered quite soon after the crash, by himself and by others. With a bit of luck, I was about to secure some pristine debris found thirty-two years earlier. Until now it had been assumed that if any extra wreckage was ever recovered it would have been degraded by the salt water over many years. These fresh pieces were like mammoth tusks, locked and preserved in the ice caps of garden sheds and attics. I sent a fax message to France on 18 October 2000 that I was en route to Wexford to visit No. 17. It was very unlikely that any previously unseen wreckage items would assist the inquiry, but they definitely had to be eliminated.

The surface of the road to Martin Connolly's home became progressively worse as I got closer. Eventually I could see St George's Channel stretching eastward to the coast of Wales. The stark profile of the lighthouse on Tuskar Rock stood watchfully, to mark the shipping hazard. I knew I was near my isolated destination, an area known locally as The Bing. Martin greeted me warmly and led me to a shed. There was no electric light within and it took a few seconds for my eyes to become accustomed to the low illumination level. He had assembled the items of wreckage on the floor (a schedule of the first collection of items recovered with the help of Martin Connolly, and with a brief description of each piece, is included as Appendix 2B). One piece in particular caught my immediate attention. I hesitated before I approached it, and with a strange feeling bordering on reverence, I stooped to pick it up. It was a section of skin from the fuselage, decorated with painted green pinstripes of the original Aer Lingus corporate colour against a geometrically arranged background of tiny grey spots, spaced at very close intervals.

In the intervening years, the marketing people at Aer Lingus have switched to a new livery, displaying a more verdant shade of green. Even the shape of the shamrock trefoil emblem was altered during an expensive revamp of the airline's brand image in the late nineties. Often, as I studied the 1970 accident report, I had tried to imagine what EI-AOM had looked like on that fateful Sunday morning as she lifted off the runway at Cork Airport. Now I was looking directly at the paler hue used in 1968, and instantly I could visualise the entire aircraft. I am sure that the full-time professionals, those whose job it is to kick their way through a million small pieces of wreckage, eventually get used to that sad task. However, as I lifted the skin of the Viscount in my hands I became acutely aware that sixty-one people had died in that airframe and I was not sufficiently battle-hardened to deal with it comfortably. I found myself mouthing a silent prayer for them.

Martin was quite happy to donate the dozen pieces of wreckage for the benefit of the French inquiry. He had even retrieved some of them from other people for that purpose. I carefully stowed a few items inside my car, placing others in the boot and on the roof rack. One of them, which looked like a hatch cover, bore a bonded aluminium label showing legible die-stamped numbers. A frame section showed evidence of failure from opposing shear forces at impact and most of the rivets had pulled clear. Incredibly, another two pieces still had rubber grommets and anti-vibration mounts in place. I looked for a priceless piece that might resemble a tailplane spar section or web plate, but my untrained eye did not see one. My sole objective now was to get the items safely into the hands of the metallurgic experts, who could evaluate their worth. Even with my scant knowledge about the world of the 'tin-kickers', I knew enough to be aware that the tedious routine of elimination is just as important in their investigations as any miraculous discovery of a diamond in the dust.

8

Neither Loud nor Clear

D uring the second week of October 2000 I spotted two errors in the 1970 report which caused some reflection on my part. With no formal training in air-crash investigation procedures I was reluctant to inform the experts that there was something amiss which did not appear to have been observed by other readers in three decades. At that time I was immersed in swan migration matters, wherein Exp'Air required specified local research. I felt that they would not take too kindly to any detour by me into areas of the study which were not really my concern. Yet it became too difficult to ignore apparent contradictions which might be helpful to them. Some days went by before I wrote to Manuel, giving a short summary of the anomaly which was mystifying me:

> I have difficulty in my mind in the reconciliation of two items.
>
> In Section 1.1 of the 1970 Report (History of the Flight) it is claimed by the authors:
>
> ATC Cork suggested that, if desired, the flight could route direct to Strumble. No direct acceptance of this suggestion was received.

At 10:40 hours (transcript of radio exchanges) Shannon called EI-AOM when it was by Youghal, climbing through 7,500 feet to FL170:

Your transmission [sic] are fairly unreadable here. Confirm you are accepting a direct routing to Strumble.

EI-AOM replied: Affirmative. Estimating Strumble at zero three.

Surely the reply by Oscar Mike indicates acceptance of direct routing?

At a later stage in the study the ETA of 11.03 GMT at Strumble Head was to take on a considerable significance. Indeed, it became quite crucial as one of a number of pointers to a contentious final conclusion by the international team.

Among the collection of documents which survive from 1970 is an innocent looking sheet which comprises an *aide-mémoire*, prepared by some person to assist the investigation team in their inquiries. It is part of a series intended to guide the team through the sequence and significance of various radio transmissions between EI-AOM and the ground stations. These old paperwork records were now in the possession of the international team in France. It was patently obvious that the memorandum in question had been used by the 1970 team, as it was still located in a prominent position on their old file. But there was something very puzzling about a discernible omission from the text of the *aide-mémoire*.

A transcript of radio exchanges with Flight 712 was prepared at Shannon Airport on 25 March 1968, the day after the crash. It was duly certified as a true copy of the audio tape. It might be expected that the exchange of signals at 10.40 hours, denoting a change in the flight plan which would enable the investigators to construct an accurate revised picture of the track of EI-AOM, would be highlighted in the *aide-mémoire* supplied to the team. The radio call from Shannon, and the affirmation in the response by the crew, was deserving of a focus. But no special attention was drawn to those transmissions by the writer of the *aide-mémoire*. In fact, it would have been impossible to highlight the signals because they do not form part of the radio transcriptions prepared for the 1970 team. The transmissions made at 10.40 hours are omitted from the text of the *aide-mémoire*. There also existed a further error of lesser significance. It was not Cork ATC which was the relevant ground station in the exchanges, as claimed in the 1970 report, but Shannon.

The time of the missing radio exchange was 10.40 hours. This four digit figure prompted me to recall the graph I had sent earlier to Exp'Air, which had included the incongruous blip in the climb profile of EI-AOM, located around the same time of 10.40. Perhaps it was all just coincidence, I thought. Yet the profound implications of the period between 10.40 and 10.43 would not allow themselves to be dismissed so lightly.

In dramatic fashion they would surface again, in a reported sighting in the skies above the townland of Old Parish, close to Helvic Head in County Waterford.

9

Devil's Advocate

———————

It was time to defect to the opposing camp. For wee
I had been pushing the case for an early minor ups
in the climb, perhaps from a bird strike. This initi
hypothesis had then expanded to embrace progressiv
degrading of the damaged tailplane skin, followed later
by failure of a spar or other critical component. It is too
easy to mount such a hobby horse, all the time ignoring
some valid pointers to an argument in favour of a sudden upset at 17,000 feet. A finding in the 1970 report said
that the Viscount had recovered from the spin described
by the pilot at 10.58 hours, and that it flew in a disabled
condition for about ten minutes. I felt a need to try
another tack, to see if a case could be made for continuity
of the spin all the way down to the sea surface, with no
recovery.

I must have read the 1970 argument for the recovery
theory at least a dozen times. Despite all my efforts to be
impartial and receptive, I had found it impossible to get
my head around the scenario of restored flight. There has
been only one occasion when a Viscount was recovered
from a spin, but that aircraft was flown by two skilled
Vickers test pilots who were exploring the limits of its
performance. The tail sustained severe distortion

uring the recovery, after the skipper E.D. Glaser was
orced to use full engine power to restore airflow on the
ail surfaces. Captain O'Beirne had a total of 6,683 flying
hours in his log-book, of which a respectable 1,679 had
been flown on Viscounts. It was unlikely that he had
engaged in any spin recovery exercises since his training
days at age twenty with the IAC.

Line pilots in command of a laden airliner approach
their tasks with consummate dedication, not allowing
any situation to develop which would expose their
aircraft to an incipient spin. This duty of care would
include avoidance of any coarse rudder inputs at the top
of the climb, especially if the airspeed was relatively
low, or if the wing angle-of-attack was high. Whatever
caused EI-AOM to snap into a vicious spin while cruising
sedately at high altitude, it was sudden, unexpected
and catastrophic. A mere thirty-three seconds after the
crew had transmitted a routine radio call to Shannon in
laconic tones, they were in distress. By now, 5,000 feet of
altitude had already been lost from the cruise level of
17,000 feet. (The original interpretation of 5,000 feet in
the final distress call had been changed to 12,000 after
acoustic analysis.) It can be calculated from the timings
that the rate of descent was in excess of 120 feet per
second, which would cause EI-AOM to hit the water
surface at about ten seconds short of 11.00 hours. This,
in fact, was the approximate time estimate provided
by no less than thirteen witnesses, who stated that they
heard a noise 'like thunder' about then.

My major difficulty with the theory of an extra ten
minutes of flight lay in the fact that I was unable to visualise how a pilot, who had failed to recover after 5,000
feet of auto-rotation and who was still spinning, would
suddenly find the answer to his dilemma in the remaining seconds. At the very instant when the pilot was first
presented with the sudden yaw of the nose to the left or

right, which invariably precedes and indeed precipitates a spin, he almost certainly immediately applied hard opposite rudder to counter the yaw, an action which would have been made by reflex, training and experience. The vertical fin, with its rudder attached, was recovered largely intact at the crash site, so it is very probable that rudder control was available. What, then, might conspire to maintain the spin? Was there also a severe pitch-down? Was the latter the initial factor?

A section of the trim tab from the right elevator, which is hinged to the tailplane, was also found at the crash site. This could indicate that the right tailplane was secure on the fuselage at the time of impact. It cannot be ignored that a portion of the spring tab from the left elevator was found on a beach seven miles from the crash site. It seems likely that the left elevator may well have detached from the aircraft, wholly or in part, before EI-AOM hit the sea. No tailplane or elevator has ever been salvaged, or even sighted by divers. A detached left elevator, perhaps even the entire left tailplane, would undeniably induce and perpetuate an irrecoverable spin to the right, and would also account for the loss of pitch control, which was apparent from the severe disintegration of the airframe on impact. Structural failure, which can lead to the detachment of a tail section, includes such possibilities as corrosion, fatigue cracks, tab flutter, failure of the rear pressure bulkhead, and bird strike.

There was another factor which contributed to my scepticism. An aircraft in a spin loses height rapidly, yet the indicated forward airspeed is always very low, hovering around the stall speed. It can be deduced from examination of the four propellers, and of the forward areas of the fuselage, that EI-AOM struck the sea at an airspeed below 130 knots, but the rate of descent was very high. The aircraft was right way up, with a slight left-wing-down tendency, indicating that the crew may have had some control of the roll axis. The fore-and-aft angle at impact was stated in the 1970 report to be about 15 degrees nose-down. All four propellers were on the flight fine pitch stops and the throttles were closed. These settings create maximum drag and it was undoubtedly a desperate attempt to reduce the impact forces. It is most unlikely that there was an attempt at a controlled ditching, particularly since the flaps were fully retracted. The undercarriage was also up, but this would be normal in a ditching.

Although I was a bit reluctant to push this alternative view, I felt that I should write to Manuel so that he could have an additional wall to bounce the ball from. With this in mind I switched into an argumentative mode and presented the best case I could muster in favour of an impact time of 11.00 hours.

Far away in Le Vesinet a file of statements was starting to accumulate on a desktop. Some new witnesses had contacted the study team and their stated observations were slowly being married to old testimony from 1968 which had been discounted as incredible at that time. The 1970 report took the view that these people must have seen later search planes. Many of the described sightings were quite bizarre. But two men, aged thirty-one and fifty-five, described a Viscount in difficulty, seen by both of them and corroborated by each other. Although their affidavits affirmed dramatic events seen in the sky from near to their homes at north Youghal, it was something else which screamed loudly for attention. The time of their sightings was about two minutes after 10.40 hours.

10

The Eccentric Cleric

———————

There comes an occasional defining moment in every relationship, when one participant takes a step which earns the respect and admiration of the other. That day came for me on 17 November 2000, when I received a very curious letter of instruction from Manuel. Until then, I had held some minor misgivings about the location of the fresh inquiry at Le Vesinet and the employment of a group of French and Australian experts. I felt it might cause that foreign team to miss some of the small details of Irish rural life as it existed in 1968. I did not really expect them to be fully conversant with the minutiae of local customs at that time, or the possible effects that they might have on the content of the witness statements. But I had misjudged the French team badly and I read Manuel's letter with mounting regard. It contained a masterly question and in a single instant I could see exactly where he was heading.

Clearly Yves and Manuel had spotted that some of the times indicated in the 1970 report were GMT, while other figures related to local time. The first fifteen pages of the report cite GMT in every case, but when an analysis of the witness statements is begun in Section 2.1.4 the report begins to refer to local time, adding a correction to GMT. At some subliminal level this changeover must have triggered a flash of inspiration among the French duo. That type of thought processing is a very desirable trait in an investigation team which is scraping the barrel for any small clue, however irrelevant it may seem at the time, and is a definitive hallmark of an open mind. This was an era before the easy availability of inexpensive and accurate mass-produced quartz watches. In fact, some people did not possess a watch at all. As a result, quite a few of the witnesses cited times of sightings or sounds as 'after Mass' or 'before dinner'. Church services were described by parishioners of the majority denomination according to the starting time, such as the 'ten o'clock Mass'. Thus the actual time of any sighting or sound observed by a witness, one who used 'after Mass' to pin down the time, might vary by one hour depending on whether the services started at GMT or according to the newly introduced Summer Time clock advance.

Now, I knew that if I could resolve the probing question posed to me by Exp'Air, it would enable the team to firm up on those times, or maybe even change the timings by a specified duration. It was essential to get detailed confirmation of the situation as it existed in 1968, and it demonstrated a very clear fact to me. Manuel's letter showed that the French had their finger firmly on the pulse of Irish rural life as it had existed in the 1960s:

… We should have a further point of interest, which could help us in reconstructing the track of the *St Phelim* prior to the crash. Should it be possible for you to check if, in March 1968, some areas in the vicinity of Fethard would have kept the local sun time, and in particular if some old priests did maintain their mass schedule according to this local sun time, which should be 30 mn late vs the national timing, which was, since February, the summer time (time zone A).

This applies in particular to the parishes of Powelford, Poulfur, Templeton.

By 22 November 2000 I had effectively found the answers they needed, and I sent my findings to Manuel.

I pointed out to him that the villages of Powelford and Poulfur, mentioned in his request, are one and the same place. The words are merely local phonetic adaptations of the original name in the Irish language, spelled differently in some witness statements. In Templetown, local parishioners confirmed to me the existence of a quaint local practice carried out some decades ago, certainly in 1970. The canon in charge of liturgical services simply refused to recognise the official introduction of Summer Time, when clocks were advanced to Greenwich Mean Time plus one hour, and referred to with the colloquial description of 'New Time'.

Masses were held in Templetown at 'Old Time', which was effectively Greenwich Mean Time. The faithful who attended services still recall the confusion it caused.

11

Scott of the Wetlands

They are a strange breed, those ornithologists. With a dedication that knows no bounds, the widow and daughter of the late Sir Peter Scott are still enthusiastically involved in a continuity of the work pioneered by him. It may be an apocryphal tale, but it is said that Scott was motivated to develop the wetlands conservation site at Slimbridge in Gloucestershire when he found a Bewick's swan near that location. It had been shot.

The 1970 report had dismissed the likelihood of a bird strike, limiting their inquiries to one species, the Greenland white-fronted goose. A possible reason for this restriction may be the fact that these flocks congregate in many thousands to feed on the Wexford sloblands, which are close to the crash site. The birds head north to breed, and away from the track of EI-AOM. But what of the Bewick's swans and the Whooper swans, feeding all over Ireland? When did they leave for their breeding grounds in Siberia and Iceland? What was their altitude? Were any of the migratory tracks in conflict with the course of EI-AOM?

I kept thinking about that other Viscount, operated by United Airlines, which had crashed, about midday, while en route from Newark to Washington six years before the Tuskar Rock disaster. It was cruising near Ellicott City when it encountered a flock of Whistling swans. The accident had occurred over land, making it easier to examine all the evidence, and to quickly establish the cause. EI-AOM, however, had plunged to the sea bed.

I contacted the Wildfowl and Wetlands Trust (WWT) near the River Severn and was steered to its Swan Office. That is the sort of office title which gladdens the heart of a researcher who is anxious to determine the migratory patterns of swans.

I gathered together as much detail as I could find, ably assisted by Jenny Earle who worked at the office, and who was a veritable fount of information on swans. She made all the records available to me and was most generous with her time and efforts. During the winter of 1967 and spring of 1968, personal computers were as scarce as hens' teeth, and of primitive design. Sir Peter Scott had diligently recorded the arrival and departure of swans in his diaries. With great foresight, Lady Philippa Scott had preserved all his old notebooks and manuscripts after his death, and these were subsequently copied on to the computer files at Slimbridge.

I assembled the data, and made a map of the outlines of our two neighbouring islands, having at this stage already acquired details of the flock concentrations of swans which spend their winter feeding regime in Ireland. I then traced the migration tracks on to the outline map, starting at points as diverse as Kerry, Cork, the Shannon estuary, and from turloughs in Galway. Using the information supplied to me by the Swan Office, I continued with the tracks toward Slimbridge, with offshoots direct to Welney in Norfolk and to Martin Mere, which is close to Southport. These are feeding stops on the routes to Siberia and to Iceland. I still lacked a final critical piece of information. It was essential to discover if flocks were still leaving Ireland as late as the crash date of 24 March, since their departures begin quite early in that month. I was particularly interested in the Bewick's swans, as their tracks were more clearly on potential collision courses with EI-AOM than the Whoopers, although the latter could not be ruled out.

I suppose that 24 March 1968 was just like any other Sunday for Peter Scott. He was blissfully unaware that the work he carried out that day would be subjected to close scrutiny in Ireland, thirty-three years later and twelve years after his death. He took careful note of the incoming swans from the west, and the departures eastward of the flocks, after they had replenished their fat reserves at the hospitable feeding grounds of the Slimbridge wetlands. Bewick's swans set course for Welney, Denmark and Siberia. The Whoopers headed north for Martin Mere and Iceland. From that old notebook I was able to ascertain that the Bewick's swans were still on the move until Wednesday 27 March 1968. The map which I completed accompanied the written data to France, and was eventually incorporated into Appendix 3a of the 2002 study. It gives a visual presentation of the movements of swans which occur every March.

As the patterns of the tracks on the map became slowly apparent, there was a disturbing confluence of the course headings. Some were crossing each other at points near Wexford and above St George's Channel. It became obvious that the flight plan filed for EI-AOM had taken the aircraft through a veritable Mig Alley of swan routes. (Mig Alley was a defined area of sky above north-western Korea, patrolled by MiG 15 jet fighters. It was there that the world's first dogfights between jets took place, when the Korean warplanes were engaged in daily combat with Sabre jet fighters of the US Air Force.) Armed with this new-found knowledge of the swan migration routes, I now turned my attention to an investigation of the likely altitudes at which the birds would fly on those journeys.

Migrating flocks of swans adopt cruise altitudes which have evolved over millennia to ensure that the greatest possible numbers of birds arrive safely at the feeding destination, or back at the breeding grounds on the reciprocal track. From above the cloud cover, celestial bodies are readily observed by them to aid navigation. The cold air reduces the risk of dehydration and the prevailing air currents are steady. The lower air density enables them to cover more distance for less energy expenditure. The basal metabolic rate of these birds is such that the reduced oxygen level and freezing air does not appear to bother them. They use three sacs on each side of their body to ingest the ram-air, with super-efficient extraction of the oxygen. In many ways they resemble modern jet airliners, which sprint skyward after takeoff to level off high above the earth.

Although the vast majority of migrating birds seem content to select a middle-of-the-road altitude for their journeys, there are always a few maverick flocks which fly higher. The radio transcripts showed that EI-AOM had been cruising at 17,000 feet, and it shocked me when I had first discovered that the record altitude for swans was a staggering 26,400 feet. As I plodded through various reference texts to see if any further data existed, I visited Richard Nairn, a wildbird guru and friend who lives close to my home, to solicit his assistance. He promised to do his best and within a week he found for me an astonishing piece of up-to-date research, which had resulted from a pooling of resources between the University of Bristol and the Icelandic Institute of Natural History in 1999. They had fitted miniature aneroid altimeters, coupled to a tiny electronic circuit, to the bodies of some Whooper swans. The circuit incorporated a transponder, and this airborne station transmitted its signals, giving location and altitude, to the Argos satellite circling the earth, from where they were relayed to a ground station. It was an imaginative and daring experiment, with no guarantee of success. The signals were intercepted with resounding accuracy. Some fascinating facts emerged, and for the very first time it was possible to determine the relationship between swans' chosen altitudes and meteorological factors such as barometric pressure patterns, air temperature, ambient sky luminosity and wind currents. The prohibitive costs of the experiment limited the number of equipped birds to six of the species, but despite this minuscule sample from the many thousands of swans, I smiled when I noticed that one of the half-dozen had climbed to 6,030 feet. I thought again of N7430, the United Airlines aircraft which crashed fatally on 23 November 1962 in Maryland, after colliding with a Whistling swan which struck the left tailplane. Like EI-AOM, that aircraft was also a Viscount. The collision occurred at 6,000 feet. It seems that the swans inhabit the skies at many different altitudes, over many countries.

Armed with my new information, in March 2001 I dashed off a brief covering memo to Exp'Air, enclosing the complete results of the Icelandic-British experiment. Perhaps Manuel might be able to compare the meteorological figures from the after-casts made in March 1968, and relate them to the way in which flight patterns of migratory birds are affected by them, as discovered through the telemetry. We knew that the Irish Bewick's swans, and possibly some Whooper flocks, were on collision courses with EI-AOM. Now it might be possible to examine their likely altitudes as well. I searched for the weather and pressure patterns of 24 March 1968 in the relevant area, and found them:

I enclose an extra 1999 study by the Icelandic Institute of Natural History, and by University of Bristol, using telemetry and the Argos satellite. This report details the effects of weather, barometric pressure, and light conditions on the altitudes and flight paths. It was only feasible to fit a small number of birds with transmitters, but despite the tiny sample it is interesting to note that one of those six swans reached 6,030 feet.

This is well below the all-time record of 26,400 feet, reported by aircrew on the same swan route on 9 December 1967, but it does illustrate the variation in altitudes, and the effects of light and barometric pressure, etc. The cruise level of EI-AOM, at 17,000 feet, was mid-way between 6,030 and 26,400 feet.

At 1100 hours on 24 March 1968 the pressure to the north-west of the British Isles was quite low, and it was high over continental Europe. The wind near Strumble Head was 210/70 at FL170, and the temperature was –23C. The QNH at Cork Airport was 998 millibars.

12

The Maintenance Fiasco

I t is an unsettling experience to peruse the findings from an analysis of the maintenance procedures on EI-AOM, a study made in secret shortly after the crash and carried out by B. O'Reilly, an inspector within the Department of Transport and Power. However, it is only proper to point out that the analysis refers to those standards which existed in 1968, and to emphasise that the quality controls employed over maintenance procedures carried out today within Aer Lingus are of the very highest standard. There were similar endemic problems worldwide in the industry at that time.

The catalyst which triggered the serious errors in the servicing strategy for the care of EI-AOM can be traced back to the changeover from Issue 1 of the plan to Issue 2 in about March 1967. This date is significant because it means that the errors were in existence for a full year before the crash date. It may help those readers who lack a forte in technical matters if we equate the situation with a family motor car, an adequate, if not a precise analogy. If you miss the manufacturer's recommended service of your Volkswagen at the next 10,000 kilometre check, the penalties are not too severe. At worst you may eventually sense a vibration in the steering wheel at cruising speed, which indicates that the front wheels are slightly out of alignment, or one wheel may have lost a lead weight balance from its rim when a kerb was struck. Perhaps the handbrake must be pulled a little more than usual to be effective. Even if the air filter is not changed, and becomes partially clogged by dust and dead flies, the car will plod on, burning an excess of fuel from the richer mixture. It is somewhat different with aircraft.

I have not used the word 'serious' to describe the mistakes without giving some thought to the matter. The analysis prepared by the inspector is a very thorough and incisive presentation. It runs to six pages. Unaided by a modern computer, he had to wade through highly complex schedules of various jobs, all arranged in the manner of a veritable minefield for the maintenance engineers. The plan was based on the guidelines issued by Vickers Armstrong, which had built the aircraft for KLM in 1957. Aer Lingus devised its own maintenance operation plan, which was approved by the relevant government department, Transport and Power.

It almost beggars belief when one first reads through the analysis report. I pride myself on a reasonable ability to absorb at least the outline and intent of such a plan, if not all the immediate details. I have spent a great part of my life tending to ships' hulls, marine engines, piston engine aircraft, ducted fan airboats, and a succession of modern and vintage cars and motorcycles. Yet when I reached the end of the analysis I was in a daze. If an airline executive had set out to be certain that Murphy's Law would feature in the plan, he could not have done better. I felt sympathy for the men on the hangar floor charged with implementing the schedules.

The details are taxing and I have limited myself to citing a few extracts from the analysis which are couched in phrases that can be easily understood. I should explain that the compliance periods between maintenance tasks for aircraft, unlike motor cars, are not calculated in kilometres. The same periods for aircraft are calculated on the hours flown, as detailed in the aircraft's log. Some items are more critical than others. For example, checking the content of oxygen bottles is important in its own right, yet any short-term neglect is unlikely to cause a crash. But failure to examine, and rectify if necessary, any excessive free play in the trim tab or spring tab attached to an elevator can have devastating consequences. If a particular compliance time is exceeded by five or ten hours it is only a marginal transgression, and a small safety buffer is taken into account when the calculation of, say, 'every 350 flying hours' is made. But at 400 hours we would be moving into a worrying time gap.

The analysis of the EI-AOM plan is replete with breaches of the compliance times. Perhaps the worst examples are on page 1 of O'Reilly's analysis, but the litany pervades the entire report. To add to the confusion, some jobs were carried out earlier than required. But it was the very late ones which held me spellbound as I read the timings, and I could not avoid wondering which particular maintenance task each appalling over-run referred to. An early definitive extract (verbatim) reads as follows, and sets the tenor for the remainder:

In the case of reverting to No.1 Inspection on Operating Plan Issue 2, having completed Inspection Nos 1 to 3 per the Initial Issue of the Operating Plan, *the following has resulted:*

All those Group Item Numbers which are in the same groups B, C, D, and E on the first and second Operating Plans have been called up as follows:
Group B: — Called *700 hours over their compliance time.*

46

Group C: — Called up within the stated compliance time.

Group D: — Called up within the stated compliance time.

Group E

ED Items — due within 350 hours, *not called until 1,400 hours.*

EE Items — due within 700 hours, *not called until 1,750 hours.*

EA Items — due within 1,050 hours, but called within 350 hours.

EB Items — due within 1,400 hours, but called within 700 hours.

EC Items — due within 1,750 hours, but called within 1,050 hours.

To gain a perspective of the implications of this extract, let us return to your family car. In urban areas a high proportion of such vehicles average about 15,000 kilometres each year, with many used only on shopping and school runs. Assume that the front brake pads may need to be replaced every year, or at the very least checked by a mechanic. Urban driving is not kind to them. Looking at the example of the ED Items within Group E, they are analogous with a situation wherein yourself, or any partner or children, were being transported in a vehicle with brakes which have not been examined for *four* years. I had a look at some typical flights of a Viscount 803 under the command of Captain O'Beirne, detailed in his log-books. Flying time on the Dublin to Liverpool sector was about forty-five minutes. Thus the maintenance overruns of 1,050 hours on the ED and EE Items equates to 1,400 flights to Liverpool, or about 800 trips to London. That is a lot of potential air mileage without the security of a well-crafted and complete maintenance schedule.

To compound the anxieties, it has not proved possible to determine the actual content of the individual job cards allocated to the various items within the plan. A thorough search of all records within Aer Lingus, the Irish Aviation Authority (IAA), and the Department of Transport and Power has proved fruitless. It is ironic that it was only the crash of EI-AOM which led to discovery of the errors during the analysis which flowed from the disaster. If the aircraft had not been lost, there appears to be no reason why the flawed plan would not have continued in its applications. No one within Aer Lingus or the Department of Transport and Power had spotted the maintenance débâcle which had existed since at least March 1967.

It crossed my mind that if the same analysis had been carried out immediately after the still unexplained loss of EI-AOF only nine months before the Tuskar Rock crash, then steps to rectify the errors could have been expedited. If that had been accomplished, then any lingering suspicions that an unknown maintenance defect could have contributed to the crash of EI-AOM would be lessened. Perhaps it took the loss of two sister ships within a short period of time to prompt the instigation of such an analysis.

Although we now know that the maintenance errors were examined by the 1970 investigation team, no mention was made of the fiasco in their final report. The man in charge of that inquiry was the same man who had authorised the annual renewal of the Certificate of Airworthiness for EI-AOM, shortly before the crash.

There are many other matters which O'Reilly brought to the attention of the department. He describes instances where the plan which related to a Viscount 808 type was applied to EI-AOM, which was an 803. A worn ribbon on an old typewriter can lead to confusion between the figures 3 and 8. At other times the Technical Planning division extended the compliance periods on some items without written authority from the Engineering people. One worker on the hangar floor altered a job card, erasing some detail which left a faint outline. At a later stage it was restored in ink by another well-intentioned engineer. He completed the task, changed his mind, and erased his signature. Many procedures were equally haphazard.

In one section of his analysis O'Reilly confirms that he informed the assistant chief inspector at Aer Lingus of his discoveries. He requested that person to investigate the use of the existing plan, not only for EI-AOM, but also for the remainder of the Viscount fleet. It was a finding within the 2002 study that the fatal training accident to EI-AOF shows remarkable similarities to the fate which befell EI-AOM, during the final twenty-five minutes of both flights. That sameness includes the flight patterns after the initial upsets and the degradation sequences. The 2002 study recommended that the file on EI-AOM should now be closed, but the team suggested that it would be of interest to reopen the file on EI-AOF. To the best of my knowledge there are no steps afoot to do this.

One thing is absolutely certain. Imagine that you are a passenger on any Aer Lingus Viscount service in 1967 or 1968. You are bowling down the runway towards takeoff speed. Through some peculiar time warp the co-pilot has managed to secure a copy of the maintenance analysis which we can access today. He proceeds to hold it in front of the skipper's nose, pointing to the ED Items. The aircraft is moving at 80 knots and you will soon be airborne. I bet my last euro that you can now sense your seatbelt protesting against severe braking forces. I would hazard a guess that, even if the aircraft is just between the decision speeds of V_1 and V_R, the takeoff will be aborted. You are now moving sideways in a ground loop, as the airport perimeter fence comes into view. In a few more seconds you will be admiring the buttercups and daisies in the meadow ahead, as the turboprop slides to a safe halt on its belly while the sheared undercarriage bogies career into a nearby paddock.

I know of no captain who would have continued the flight.

13

Conflict of Interest

There are hard questions to be asked about the level of adherence to maintenance schedules, and some which concern other matters, in the conduct of Aer Lingus or the Department of Transport and Power as they existed in 1968. Computers had not yet arrived, and records were kept on individual, handwritten job cards. Mechanics were drawn from non-aviation backgrounds and given training. Some individuals from the motor trade or from CIE, the national road and rail transport company, may well have lacked punctiliousness, a trait so essential in aircraft maintenance. This weakness may have been mirrored by a casual attitude to the importance of accurate paperwork and record-keeping.

The temerity to raise these points against a government department and our national flag carrier may be viewed by some as tantamount to treason. Like most Irish people, I am proud of the humble beginnings of our airline, spawned by the small De Havilland biplane *Iolar* as she battled headwinds on the first flights to and from Bristol. The postwar fleet of the ubiquitous DC-3 aircraft was joined by the Viscounts. The former has familiar engines with pistons, cylinders, spark plugs and valves. When production ceased in 1947, the Douglas aircraft company had built a total of 10,654 civil and military variants of the DC-3. A further 2,500 of the type were built under licence in Japan and the USSR. It was an extremely robust and reliable design and all of its maintenance quirks were very well known within the aviation industry. Most of the work could be carried out with a modest toolbox and some torque wrenches. Astonishingly, although the type entered service with American Airlines on 25 June 1936, flying the New York–Chicago overnight sleeper route, there are quite a few DC-3 aircraft still in service today. Irreverent Australian pilots who flew it claimed that the wing main spar was 'built like a brick shithouse', an inspired comparison with the shanty 'dunny' built of timber outside antipodean homesteads.

But the Viscount was a different ball game, a new design powered by turbine engines and with a pressurised hull which climbed above the weather. It was fast, roomy and comfortable. The marketing gurus at Aer Lingus carried out demonstration trips to invited groups, and the media was most impressed by the trick of standing a coin on its edge in the vibration-free cabin. The pilots loved it too. Yet we now know from the long litany of airworthiness directives which began to appear shortly after its introduction, and which continued into the 1990s, that it may have been a goodly apple rotten at the core. A high proportion of the mandatory notices to airlines from the safety authorities relate to fatigue cracks, corrosion, and incipient failures within the tail area. I constructed a sample of fourteen such directives from the Federal Aviation Authority (FAA) in the US, issued between 1955 and 1995, all tail-related and critical. These extracts make up Appendix 3b of the 2002 study and give a feel of the complex difficulties faced by the maintenance division of any airline with a Viscount fleet. An apt phrase which springs to mind is 'intensive care'.

In retrospect there was something very odd about an airline which invited clerics to sprinkle holy water on each fuselage during the annual blessing of the fleet at Dublin Airport. The sobriquet chosen for the naming of EI-AOM was *St Phelim*. That saint's name was inscribed on the front of the aircraft, which became the first part of the Viscount to strike the sea surface close to Tuskar Rock. Concurrent with this almost Druidic liturgy, errors had crept into the Maintenance Plan for Viscounts. Some tasks were now being executed by men in overalls at periods which exceeded the compulsory compliance time by a factor of four, as indicated in page 37 of the 1999 review. Men in suits, who were charged with ensuring that the maintenance plan was strictly followed, failed to spot the errors for more than a year.

As each section of wreckage was recovered from the sea bed, it was transported on army trucks to a hangar at Casement Aerodrome, Baldonnel. Lawyers acting for some members of the crew and for some passengers sought access for a technical inspection of the partial reconstruction of the airframe. This was denied by citing the Air Regulations of 1957, and by claiming that the investigation was a private matter for the minister responsible. Contemporaneous Aer Lingus and government memoranda which are now available for scrutiny reveal that shortly after the 1970 report was published a proposal was made to place a notice in newspapers inviting interested parties to re-apply for inspection of the wreckage. The notice was prepared in draft form, but after some internal discussions the decision was reversed.

On 25 November 1970 the Inspector of Accidents wrote to Aer Lingus, releasing the wreckage into its custody. In his letter he claimed that none of the previously interested parties had been in contact again. But how could they, after the decision was made to cancel the notice of invitation? It was agreed by the airline that it would retain the remains of the aircraft until January, in case any third parties wished to examine them. Yet, with indecent haste, Aer Lingus scrapped the wreckage shortly after it came into its possession, claiming afterwards that this action was inadvertent. There is no record of the method of disposal. It may have ended up in landfill, or far out to sea. It could have been melted down into ingots for the scrap metal trade in aluminium and alloys. When it disappeared, no third party had ever been allowed to examine any section of it.

The man who released the wreckage was the same man who had approved renewal of the Certificate of Airworthiness on EI-AOM for a further year. That document is dated 14 February 1968, only 38 days before the crash. The issue of this important safety certificate was not accompanied by any actual examination of the aeroplane in physical terms. Instead of this, only the paperwork was examined. If this showed that the aircraft had been maintained during the previous year with strict adherence to the plan schedules as approved by the department, then a fresh certificate was issued. But the serious errors in the maintenance strategy were not spotted by department staff at the time of issue of the new certificate. They were only discovered during their review of procedures after the disaster.

There exists a further disturbing element. An internal Aer Lingus memo dated 3 January 1968 was sent from 'MSS' (Management Support Services?) to the chief inspector. It was signed 'J. Butler' and reveals that the work cards from an important check dubbed 'Inspection Visit 2.04', claimed by him to have been carried out on 17 and 18 December 1967, were missing. It is puzzling that when the licensed engineer who had signed off the 2.04 inspection was asked for a report *after the crash*, he gives the date of the inspection as 19 December 1967, and not the dates indicated by 'J. Butler'. This anomaly emphasises the inherent risks when there is a reliance solely on memory. The engineer's report is dated 2 April 1968, with no addressee, and is signed 'F. Begley'. It carries his Engineer's Licence number 85ACX. He states that 'to the best of my recollection' there were no carry-over defects associated with the 2.04 inspection. The records that would certify that all aspects of the 2.04 check were completed had been lost and were never received in the Quality Control Records office within the airline. They would have included a copy of the Maintenance Release. The memo from 'J. Butler' admits that the complete 2.04 work package was missing. A pre-requisite for renewal of the Certificate of Airworthiness was an affirmation that all such documents relating to the maintenance history of EI-AOM were in order. In the preamble above his initials, which are scribed in his capacity as 'Aeronautical Officer' within the department, the man who subsequently headed the team of crash investigators verified approval of the certificate renewal:

I certify:
(a) that all recommendations made by the Inspecting Officers have been satisfactorily performed;
(b) that all compulsory modifications or alterations applicable to this type of aircraft have been incorporated;
(c) that this aircraft is on this day in good and air-worthy condition and is recommended for continuation of Certificate of Airworthiness;
(d) that the aircraft documents are in order.

Not only had the department staff failed to notice the serious errors which had developed during the changeover from Issue 1 of the Maintenance Plan to Issue 2, but there was now certification of the validity of

Inspection Visit 2.04 on 19 December 1967, despite the fact that all save one of the job cards relating to that check had been lost. Those records were not found before the crash, and remain missing to this day. To make matters worse, it has not proved possible to establish the contents of the list of tasks embraced by the 2.04 check. The further discharge of duties carried out by the man who had approved the Certificate of Airworthiness, and who had released the wreckage to Aer Lingus, was an obvious conflict of interest. (Such a conflict could not occur today. On 1 January 1994 the IAA was set up. The AAIU is a separate entity. The latter operates at arm's length with a very independent structure. Its reports are prepared in strict accordance with the terms set out within Annex 13 of the International Civil Aviation Organization Convention, and the professionalism of the AAIU is recognised worldwide. All its reports are textbook examples of precision and detail.) The findings of his final report concerning the crash were presented by him on 30 June 1970. On that occasion he acted in his capacity as Inspector of Accidents, which appears below his signature on the report.

One would expect that so important a matter as the errors in the maintenance schedules, or mention of the missing 2.04 records, would have figured prominently in the body of the 1970 report or in the appendices. The maintenance history of an aircraft, particularly when the crew reported that it was 'spinning', would normally be investigated and reported on in considerable detail. There is, however, a resounding silence on all these aspects of the crash within the report.

While there is no evidence that the defects in the record-keeping systems employed by Aer Lingus contributed to the initial upset from failure in the area of the left tailplane, it is a worthwhile exercise to discover if there are any accidents where similar shortcomings were responsible. One such typical example occurred on 8 June 1995 at Atlanta. During the takeoff roll of a ValuJet flight to Miami, a loud bang was heard and the crew of a following aircraft informed the pilot of the DC-9 by radio that he had a visible engine fire. The takeoff was aborted immediately, but shrapnel from the exploded engine had penetrated a fuel line, which sprayed burning kerosene and started a fire in the rear of the passenger cabin. All sixty-two persons on board escaped the flames by scrambling to safety through the forward doors and the over-wing exits. It was found that a small fatigue crack had developed from a tiny corrosion pit in the engine compressor. The crack had grown slowly until the disc ruptured. The 'Probable Cause' in the NTSB accident report (AAR-96/03) carries a salutary warning for all who neglect maintenance paperwork:

> The lack of an adequate record-keeping system and the failure to use process sheets to document the step-by-step overhaul and inspection procedures contributed to the failure to detect the crack and, thus, to the accident.

14

The Escape above Parkes

For my sins, I am the type of person who often mentally files away bits of trivia which other more sensible mortals erase from their memory bank. It was for this reason that some recollections from my earlier years in Australia surfaced again in June 2001. I felt that their possible relevance to the inquiry demanded at least a mention to the French investigation team. I had to rely on memory, as neither of the recalled incidents was of sufficient importance in the annals of aviation to be readily verified. Yet I had no doubt that details of both occurrences lie within dusty Department of Civil Aviation files somewhere in Sydney. If Colin Torkington felt that the control lock incident merited any closer examination, then he would no doubt have the right contacts among his old Aussie mates to secure a copy of the file without too much difficulty.

Jamming of the primary flight controls on the ill-fated Viscount was always a possible cause of the crash and consistent with the known facts. Only small sections of the various control runs, with nothing to reveal, had been recovered at the crash site. I knew that Exp'Air probably did not have the time or the budget to pursue too many extra avenues of inquiry. None the less I felt compelled to send some brief notes to Manuel, particularly about the little-known and almost fatal Fokker Friendship incident above Parkes in New South Wales. During the last week of June 2001, I assembled four extra notes for Manuel, and despatched them to France:

Note 1: Foreign Objects
Two of the FAA directives on Viscounts relate to a risk from foreign objects jamming the primary flight controls. These could enter via the cockpit floor, or through holes in the control column housings where unnecessary metal is excised to reduce weight. (See directives of 6 July 1959 and 9 February 1969.) I can recall only one fatal occasion when this unusual type of accident occurred. In the late 1960s, or early 1970s, an instructor and his pupil died during a spin recovery training exercise near Bankstown Airport in Sydney. The De Havilland Chipmunk was seen to descend in a fully developed state of auto-rotation, near the training area at Hoxton Park.

The rotation was stopped with rudder, but the aircraft did not pull out of the pitch-down attitude, and it hit the ground. There was much mystery about the accident, as the instructor was a veteran of 617 Dambusters Squadron, and was very experienced. The investigators eventually found a distorted Australian 20 cent coin jammed in the bellcrank of the elevator controls. At some period beforehand, a trainee pilot had neglected to remove coins from his pocket before aerobatics. The joystick was bent backwards by desperate attempts to pitch up.

Note 2: Control Lock
The Airworthiness Directive of 10 July 1958, relating to aileron lock arm/locking lever clearances on Viscounts, reminded me of another Australian

incident, also involving a Dart-engine turboprop like EI-AOM. A Fokker Friendship, of either East-West Airlines or Airlines of New South Wales, was en route above the town of Parkes. After the top of the climb the skipper engaged the autopilot, and pushed his seat back to stretch his legs. Behind the seat, a manual with a thick protective cover was pushed backwards by the seat movement, and it silently engaged the control lock by pushing on the lock lever which was located on the rear cockpit bulkhead. The crew did not immediately identify the cause of the subsequent roll problems, and they attempted to control the aircraft by picking up each downgoing wing with asymmetric power applications.

The Fokker descended from 14,000 feet in increasing roll oscillations. Finally the crew were forced to close one throttle, and to pick up the opposite wing with full power. The next roll called for full power on the idling engine, but there is apparently a safety feature on the F-27 which saved the aircraft and all on board. When the control lock is selected, only one throttle at a time is free to be advanced beyond 12,800 rpm. The Throttle Lock Selector is located on the rear of the central pedestal, and permits the choice of which throttle lever is free to move. Because the selected throttle would not advance, the skipper then immediately spotted his problem, and disengaged the control lock at 2,000 feet. He recovered the aircraft. *I mention the foregoing incident to you for the following reasons:*

(a) The 1970 Report [Appendix 11.9] stated that 'the lever in the pedestal was in the stowed position (i.e. locks off)'. Agreed, this was its position *at impact*. But it could have been 'On' at an earlier stage of the flight. In fact, if the crew of the F-27 detailed above had not spotted their problem until a minute or so later, they would have disengaged the lock at too low an altitude for recovery. There would have been an unsolved accident, because the wreckage would reveal that the lock was in the *safe* position. The crash investigators would have no method to determine that the lever was only moved to the safe position just before ground impact, unless a Cockpit Voice Recorder tape revealed a last-minute crew exclamation that the lock was engaged, or if a Flight Data Recorder told the story. There was no CVR or FDR on EI-AOM.

(b) Such a hypothesis would fit in with that most unusual radio transmission from EI-AOM at 1058.02 hours: 'Echo India Alpha Oscar Mike ... with you.' It is delivered in an uncommon radio style, which could indicate that they had an incipient problem developing at that time. A roll excursion is not incompatible. Eight seconds later they were spinning.

(c) The same hypothesis also reconciles with the evidence that the filament in the illuminating bulb of a Fasten Seat Belt sign failed 'hot' from high-G forces, i.e. it was 'on' at impact. Some passenger seat belts were also fastened [Appendix 4a of 1970]. It is possible that an unusual and rapidly deteriorating situation could have prompted the crew to switch on the sign. Sudden catastrophic tail damage would surely focus crew minds to an intense level, which would exclude thoughts of No Smoking signs.

I have no knowledge of the design and location of the control lock lever on a Viscount 803 pedestal, or whether there is any possible unusual chain of circumstances which could lead to its accidental engagement, as happened on the Australian F-27.

Neither do I know whether or not there is any significance in the Mandatory AD issued by Vickers and FAA on 10 July 1958, requiring that the locking levers should be filed to obtain a clearance of 0.15 inch between the aileron lock arms and their associated locking levers.

It might be worthwhile to have a look at the remote possibility of a control lock problem. I do not think that the 1970 report considered the possibility at all, simply because the lever was safe *at impact.*

Note 3: Elevator Tab Flutter

My attention was grabbed by an Associated Press news report on 4 June 2001, stating that a workhorse aircraft type had lost a piece of an elevator tab in flight. I searched the American files, and discovered that an Emergency Airworthiness Directive was recently issued by the FAA, on 24 April 2001. This requires all operators of more than 1,000 older 737 types to look for improperly fitted jam nuts. An incorrect torque force on the nuts was applied at the Seattle factory, when the control rod length was rigged by Boeing. This can lead to elevator tab 'flutter', and can cause loss of control in the aircraft.

I only mention it because of the severed 18-inch section of the elevator spring tab from EI-AOM, which was found near Greenore Point, seven miles from the crash site.

I attach the full AD, in case it is of any interest to you.

Note 4: Tailplane & Elevator Cracks, Corrosion, Fatigue

There is a disproportionately high number of Airworthiness Directives concerned with Viscount tailplanes. The spread involves the earlier 700 series and the later 800 types.

A very short time after the type entered service, the first AD appears on 24 April 1955.

This relates to cracks already found in the tailplane centre section mainspar. These cracks appear along the lines of rivets attaching the web plate.

In 1957, following buckling of a tailplane, the thickness of the skin was increased to 18 SWG [Standard Wire Gauge]. Then a new placard was mandated to be placed in view of the pilot, requiring reduced turbulence penetration speed to avoid tailplane stresses.

Nine days before the crash of EI-AOM, a new AD was issued on 15 March 1968 concerning fatigue cracks in the root joint fittings of top spars on Viscount tailplanes. In 1994 the FAA advised that accumulated in-service experience has shown that the newer Viscount 800 series were more prone to tailplane fatigue cracks than the 700 type, because some spar fittings bore higher stress levels. EI-AOM was an 803.

On 15 August 1995 the FAA issued another AD, after cracking and corrosion was discovered in the mainspar forward booms and upper root joints. There are also at least nine ADs relating to the elevators on Viscounts, which cite corrosion, fatigue, quilting, delamination, and latent jamming or control run problems. In addition, there were also numerous aileron problems.

The aft area of the empennage of this dihedral-tail Vickers Viscount design seems to have been prone to particular weaknesses, some of which may have been shared by the similar Vickers Vanguard design. One of the latter type crashed in Belgium, killing all aboard, after the rear pressure bulkhead failed due to undetected corrosion hidden at the interface of a bonded doubler. The sudden pressure rise within the tail cone blew off the tailplane skin panels, with loss of pitch control. In that instance the cause was immediately established because the crash site was on land. The same bulkhead on EI-AOM was constructed in a similar way. It is not of much safety importance today because few, if any, Viscounts are in service. But what was the significance in 1968?

I have written a separate note to you on the ADs which relate to the corrosion problems in the rear of the pressure hull, including the area beneath the dorsal fin, and in the aft pressure bulkhead. That bulkhead, located near Frame 87.1, was not recovered at the crash site, and no parts of it were ever seen or found.

I kept wondering about the significance of some corrosion repairs carried out on EI-AOM by Scottish Aviation at Prestwick, when the aircraft was sold to Aer Lingus by KLM. The Dutch airline had flown it in service for ten years. Some belly skin panels were entirely replaced, and it would be relevant to the study if they were located anywhere near Frame 87.1, in the tail area. The very experienced maintenance engineers of British European Airways (BEA) had failed to detect the hidden corrosion which downed the Vickers Vanguard G-APEC over Belgium. In fact, it was impossible for them to spot any evidence until the intergranular rot had worked its way through to the rear surface of the bonded doubler. Urine spilled in the toilet area had contaminated the bilge, and attacked the bulkhead from below, because of a drain hole blocked by an excess of a local sealant paste.

By coincidence I had personal experience of similar contamination in the steel hull of an elderly passenger ferry which I commanded in the 1990s. At her annual safety survey in 1997, the vessel was inspected at

Alexandra Basin in Dublin Port. A cautious and dedicated surveyor from the local Marine Survey Office at
Eden Quay was wary of an ultrasound test, which
showed that the thickness of the steel plates still
retained integrity. He required me to sandblast away all
the repeated applications of anti-foul paint, and the
black ship's paint which extended below the waterline,
to reveal the original metal surface. The high-pressure
sand jets did their work and at first everything looked
fine. Then we arrived at the aft area of the starboard side
where, to my utter disbelief, the nozzle stream of high
velocity sand cut straight through corroded wafer-thin
metal. Directly above this affected area of the hull was a
toilet, and there was evidence that some limber holes
in the bilge were now blocked by flaked rust. It was
immediately apparent from the location of the corroded
area that urine, which had spilled into the hidden bilge,
had contributed to acceleration of the damage. The
ship's passenger certificate was withdrawn by the
marine authority, and I spoke to Michael Klyne and
Chris Uglow, two experienced surveyors involved in
the inspection. They had a few words of advice for me:

> Never place total trust in an ultrasound test. You
> have to crawl in there, where everything is dark and
> dirty, and eyeball the scene. Low-tech methods work
> best where safety is involved. Always bring a
> hammer, and don't be afraid to hit the plates hard if
> you are in any doubt. You soon learn the correct
> sound made by the right metal thickness.

Male passengers standing in the unfamiliar cramped
surroundings of a Viscount toilet can understandably
lose directional control of a urine stream, particularly in
mild turbulence. The excess which misses the toilet
bowl must eventually find its way to another area, and

if this happens regularly over a long period it is certain to have a cumulative effect. Surface slop from liquids in the waste tank, leaky fittings, or careless emptying procedures may be contributory factors. The problem is exacerbated by the common practice of imbibing lots of beer, coffee and other diuretics by airline passengers.

The new external skin panels fitted to the underbelly of EI-AOM at Prestwick certainly looked nice, and added to the aesthetics of the outward appearance. At the back of my mind a few questions intruded. Was a toilet located anywhere near the area of the new skin panels? Were the affected panels in the vicinity of Frame 87.1, which is close to the rear bulkhead of the pressure hull? (I discovered in January 2002 that the replaced skin panels had in fact been located in the rear area of the fuselage, which placed them close to Frame 87.1. Although ominous, no conclusion was possible because of a lack of supportive evidence.) What inspection methods were used by Aer Lingus to detect corrosion at the interface of any doubler plate, if one existed? Were these methods superior to the Maintenance Plan employed by BEA, whose engineers had failed in 1971 to detect the fatal infection of G-APEC? When the BEA fleet was inspected after the Belgium crash, it was found that other sister ships were similarly affected. The accident report reveals that BEA failed to notify the aircraft manufacturers of the discoveries, and the airline simply introduced a revised detection schedule.

Likely as not, the corrosion on the panels which were replaced on EI-AOM was probably quite superficial, and may have only amounted to a few small spots here and there. There is, of course, a frightening analogy which can be drawn with those corrosion spots, in the field of medicine. The onset of bacterial meningitis is heralded by spots on the skin. The problem is that these blotches do not usually appear until the underlying infection has already taken a firm hold, and they are often the final symptom. Radical intervention is urgently required at this stage, but it does not take the form of a skin graft to beautify the patient's appearance. The spots will never kill you, but the septicaemia assuredly will.

15

Not a Sparrow shall Fall

The seasonal activities of Christmas 2000 provided a welcome short break from the small rectangular world of my PC screen. By now I had been living in front of that piece of wizardry for almost three months, trawling the distant Internet archives of the National Transportation Safety Board (NTSB) in the US and other such worldwide agencies. These organisations have diligently stored information on the aetiology of the various diseases which afflicted the fleets of Viscounts since the 1950s, particularly within the Americas. The sales team at Vickers had successfully exploited the novel attributes of the world's first turboprop airliner, and they made great strides in market penetration of the USA when Capital Airlines placed an order for sixty Viscounts.

I went through the motions of festive cheer and the New Year celebrations, having promised my family that I would put the 1968 disaster out of my mind for ten days. This was easier said than done. There is an obsessive factor attached to this type of research, and I often wonder how career investigators manage to hold their personal relationships on an even keel in the face of these compulsions. The unsolved questions never really go away, except for an hour or so.

With the start of the New Year of 2001, fresh avenues of inquiry were begun in France. Some curious sightings above County Wexford had been reported by witnesses on the day of the Tuskar crash. They were inexplicable in aviation terms, and bordered on the bizarre. One person, located at Saltmills, which is about two miles north of Fethard, described 'three black clouds' in the vicinity of an aircraft which was 'unsteady and descending'. Another observer, at Grange, about one mile north of Fethard, also described a black cloud and an aeroplane which seemed to be enveloped in a haze, which he described as 'about the size of a large hayshed'. This mist was revolving and travelling with the aircraft. Shortly afterwards, the witness heard a loud bang which died away like thunder. The 1970 report considered that these events could be satisfactorily explained by the presence of a supersonic military aircraft coming out of a dive, which caused a sonic boom and the small clouds. It then flew past the witness with the wing covered in condensation shimmer, which is typical of an aircraft flying through humid air at near-sonic speed. Television viewers will often see this same occurrence during a Grand Prix motor race. In some weather conditions this shimmer, together with tip vortices, can be clearly seen on the inverted wing which is employed to increase down force and tyre grip at the rear of the racing car. It was this theory of a supersonic bang, and other similar suggestions in the report, which fed rumours of the existence of a second aircraft, guided missile, or target drone, which had collided with EI-AOM. The Viscount was excluded from the equation because its radio signals showed that it was close to the coast of Wales at this time, at 17,000 feet.

It would be too much of a burden for the average non-technical reader to follow the sequence of discoveries which led to an entirely different explanation for the small black clouds and the swirling mist which accompanied the rogue aircraft. Thus I will limit myself to a very simple description, in the knowledge that any reader who is an expert on fuel control units and negative gravitational (g) forces will fill in the gaps for themselves.

In the simplest terms, *positive* g force is experienced at a fun fair just when the rider on a roller-coaster reaches the bottom of a steep incline and travels upward again. The sensation is felt in the buttocks as they are pushed down into the seat. When the rider reaches the top of the next high-speed apex prior to another descent, the force acts in a different direction and will be felt in the shoulders which are restrained by a bar or harness. This is *negative* g, a force which occurs during some deliberate aerobatic manoeuvres, such as at public flying displays. It can also happen during attempts by an airline pilot to recover an aircraft which has suffered an upset from some unforeseen cause. In addition, severe air turbulence, however brief, can reproduce the same phenomenon. There are many instances where unbelted passengers have struck the cabin ceiling during turbulence. The same negative force can also upset the normal operation of some sensitive parts on the aircraft itself.

Lateral thinking is an expression which is frequently bandied about by philosophers, mathematicians, astronomers, and others of their ilk. As an art form, lateral thinking is best seen in the mindsets of people like Copernicus, who asked a very simple question which was later endorsed by Galileo. What if it is the earth which moves around the sun, and our planet is not the centre of the universe? In its modern application that same question is often posed to a lesser degree by the great successful air crash investigators of our day, such as Greg Feith of the NTSB, and his colleague Bob McIntosh. In the UK, Bob Nelson and Bill Houghton were also consummate lateral thinkers among many others. If we now apply their rule of thumb, we are forced to ask an obvious question: *What if the Viscount was not near the coast of Wales at all, and the aircraft observed near Fethard was indeed EI-AOM?* Is there any likely scenario which would produce the strange reported symptoms of small black clouds, a swirling mist which accompanied the flight path, and yet one which might also fit in with a statement by another witness that one of the propellers was stopped and 'bent'? A person who is unfamiliar with the feathering process of a propeller might readily describe the appearance of the blades in that position as 'bent'.

A new witness, who was traced by AAIU, has described an erratic path by an aircraft at very low altitude. He is convinced that it was a Viscount and he was able to read letters on its side. It approached the field where he was feeding cattle, as if to land. It broke off the approach in a right turn and climbed. After three or four minutes of ascent it suddenly dived again, spinning to the right above the Kennedy Arboretum. If it was EI-AOM, it is likely that the required desperate measures by the crew to recover from the abrupt spin or spiral dive may have exacerbated any existing damage to the tail. Outside Ballykelly Church, as he emerged after Mass, a witness saw an aircraft so low that he recognised the windows, colours and even the registration letters of a Viscount. The climb after the dive, and the push-over at the top as EI-AOM regained flying speed on a parabolic path, bears similarities to the roller-coaster analogy. A brief period of negative g forces may have been induced on the aircraft. If that is true, it behoves us to look very closely at what Rolls-Royce have to say in its Manual of Operating Instructions for the Dart engines fitted to Viscounts. The message is blunt: Negative 'g' manoeuvres should be avoided where possible, *as this may cause automatic feathering of the propellers* (my italics).

We now have a possible explanation for the 'bent' blades observed by a witness on engine number 3. But what about the three black clouds? The fuel control unit on Viscounts is also known to be sensitive to unusual acceleration forces, and it is possible that it delivered an uncontrolled fuel flow to three of the four engines. The result of this would be three black clouds emitted in the vicinity. Having exceeded the design limitations in the stressful recovery, it is also possible that the fuel system and tanks, or the water methanol reservoirs, suffered rupture at one or more points, perhaps through partial disconnection of a pipe under load from lateral acceleration in the spin. In fact, when sections of the fuel plumbing were examined after they were lifted from the sea bed, it was found that the starboard valve from the refuelling system was partly open. Such ruptures or failures would explain the swirling mist which accompanied the aircraft and create a credible alternative to the 1970 belief that the sightings were that of a near-sonic military machine in humid air. It is also worth remembering that all of these sightings occurred shortly before the final plunge into the sea, seen by two independent witnesses. The Viscount was already in its death throes at this time.

As in all such hypotheses, you search desperately for any other small clue to support the theory. It was to come in the most unexpected guise of a pigeon fluttering to earth. The statement to police by a farmer at Gorteens, close to Fethard, reveals that the bird landed in his garden shortly after the sighting of the mobile haze by a different witness. Its entire body was covered in some unusual liquid. If it was oil, the bird was certain to die unless there was some intervention by way of detergent cleansing. It avoided capture, and stayed in the garden for a few days to recuperate. The liquid remained on the bird during the day of the crash, but by the next day it had started to disappear and a few short flights were possible. The curious farmer continued to observe the bird at intervals, and the pigeon flew away after three or four days. The liquid had to be volatile, certainly not oil, to evaporate in this manner in the low ambient air temperatures of March.

There is one liquid which meets all those criteria. It is JP-1, a high-grade form of aviation kerosene fuel, used to power the Dart turboprop engines of Flight 712. Although less volatile than petrol, JP-1 will evaporate in a few days. Did the pigeon fly through an airborne blanket of fuel mist which escaped from ruptured fittings on EI-AOM? Did it eventually decide on a forced landing in the farmer's garden, when its wings lost their aerodynamic lift through saturation of the flight feathers by kerosene?

There is no mention of the distressed bird in the examination of witness sightings in the 1970 report (Sec. 2.1.4). Yet the statement was, and still is, on file, and it seems reasonable to suggest that the timing of its fall to earth, which coincided with the strange sightings in the skies overhead, should have warranted a close scrutiny of the incident.

16

Shades of Dorian Gray

As the springtime of 2001 drew to a close the conclusions which would ultimately form the official findings of the 2002 study had gelled. It was now a matter of fine-tuning them, and conducting a trawl of any remaining peripheral suspicions which had not reached the exhaustion stage of analysis. Among the latter, one suspect had not been fully eliminated from the faces at the identity parade. The pressure hull of EI-AOM was still standing mute in that line-up.

I did promise at the start of this book that I would strive to provide a simple pathway through those technical aspects which are sometimes unavoidable in a work of this nature. It is for this reason that we shall be talking about the coffee jar in your kitchen, a slow puncture in your car tyre, and jam sandwiches.

Those who flew in aircraft of the DC-3 era will remember the tray of wrapped sweets offered by a smiling air stewardess to her charges, just before take-off. This act of generosity was aimed toward passenger comfort, and not simply at titillation of the palate. As the DC-3 climbs to its cruise altitude, where air pressure is lower than at sea level, the trapped air inside eardrums naturally increases in volume. The expansion exerts pressure within the ear, causing discomfort and reduced hearing. In extreme cases pain may be felt, which can also emanate from cavities within the bone structure of the skull, particularly if the sinus drainage is blocked by symptoms of the common cold or by an infection. Driving a car in mountain areas can produce a similar effect to a lesser degree, and a descent to the lowlands can lead to a 'popping' in the ears as the pressure is equalised again. By sucking on a sweet, the act of swallowing has a secondary effect which helps to maintain that equilibrium. After some time spent climbing, the piston engines on the DC-3 would eventually be starved of air for the fuel mixture in the thinning atmosphere and run out of puff. And like the crews of combat aircraft in the Second World War, every passenger would need an oxygen mask shortly after they had climbed through 10,000 feet.

Aircraft manufacturers who sought to ply the skies at high altitude where profits are also higher, conjured up a solution to these problems. When we can fly high, we eliminate jarring discomforts from air turbulence, delays and diversions due to weather, the hazards of mountains, and the need to detour around towering cumulonimbus thunderheads which contain threats to safety. In addition, pure jet engines and turbine-driven propeller engines are much more efficient at high altitude, and fuel costs are reduced. The answer was to make the hull of the aircraft as airtight as your kitchen container for fresh coffee grounds, and to pressurise the interior with pumps which are balanced by an adjustable outflow of the air through valves. This can be compared to a driver pumping up a car tyre which has a slow puncture or a faulty valve. As the airliner climbs after takeoff, the outflow valves are kept closed, allowing the pumps to increase the pressure within the cabin. This equates to a 'lower' and more comfortable altitude.

The flight crew is able to control the ascent rate by this artificial means, allowing you to experience a slow climb. In real terms at this time the aeroplane is rocketing skyward. During descent for the landing, the rate experienced by the passengers is equally kind.

The provision of all this passenger comfort brings with it some unique problems for aircraft design teams. The structure must be built to withstand a 'differential' pressure, say, for example, 6 pounds per square inch (6 psi). This means that the cabin skin can maintain an interior pressure which is 6 psi greater than the atmosphere outside the aircraft. You may see occasional disaster movies when a window or other part of the aircraft ruptures and everything in the vicinity is sucked out. This happens very rarely and we are familiar with the pre-flight demonstration by cabin staff showing how to breathe by using the personal oxygen masks which automatically deploy from above you. The pilot will dive the aircraft to a lower altitude where normal breathing resumes. You may also notice that aircraft doors open inwards and are sealed in place by the internal pressure. Windows are also specially designed.

Stress is induced on the hull every time it expands a little from pressurisation, and when it contracts during depressurisation. Regular inspection and maintenance is essential to ensure that the integrity of the pressure hull is never compromised by damage from corrosion, fatigue cracks or other causes. In November 2000 I had written to Exp'Air about a Vickers Vanguard accident above Belgium on 7 October 1971. The BEA aircraft suffered failure of the rear bulkhead because of undetected corrosion. As the air from inside the pressurised hull rushed out through the tail cone at 19,000 feet, it briefly raised the pressure inside the tailplane skins, blasting them from the skeletal structure of spars and ribs. The aircraft plunged to earth killing all on board. The same manufacturers, Vickers, also built the Viscount, which shared some common design features with its bigger sister, particularly in the tail area.

I eventually discovered that the Viscount did not have a doubler plate on its rear pressure bulkhead. It was this method of construction which had hidden the growing corrosion at the interface of two bonded plates on the Vanguard. If you can visualise a jam sandwich, then the bread is like the two plates, while the jam represents the corrosion. At first nothing is visible. After some time the jam will seep through the bread or reach the crust area, plain to see. Unfortunately, in the analogy with aircraft maintenance, the bulkhead will fail before you can see the jam, and it did so in 1971.

Although I had arrived in a cul-de-sac when I discovered that the Viscount bulkhead did not have a doubler plate, I kept hunting in the archives in an effort to determine if any other weakness could be present in that area of EI-AOM. I was startled to uncover some data which indicated that there had existed more than one threat to the pressure hull. I sent the details post-haste to France. By February of 1970, twenty-three months after the crash of EI-AOM, it was established that the pressure hulls of both 700 and 800 series Viscounts had been under threat from corrosion. The first airworthiness directive became effective on 22 February 1970, following reports of breakdown of the protective paint beneath the dorsal fin and corrosion of the hidden fuselage skin. One section of the corrective actions called for removal of the complete dorsal fin, repairs to the damage, resealing, and repainting. On 20 August 1971 a further AD was issued, this time solely in relation to the 800 series, the family to which EI-AOM belonged. This called for an immediate reduction of the cabin pressure differential to 4.5 psi for aircraft which had accumulated 20,000 landings, with a further reduction to 3.5 psi at 25,000 landings. Operators were required to inspect the suspect rear pressure bulkhead boundary member for cracks and to conduct appropriate repairs. This AD had been issued only six weeks before the failure of the Vanguard bulkhead. By 1991 there were further corrosion and crack problems with the rear and forward face of the rear pressure bulkhead, and with the web lap-joints. The same boundary members indicated in the very first AD, and the adjacent fuselage skin, were also fingered again. Additional ADs and amendments were issued in each case.

On the covers of the travel brochures and timetables which survive from the 1950s there are superb pictures of the Viscount turboprop. Those earlier black-and-white portraits changed to flattering colour images during the course of the 1960s, and the aircraft seemed ageless, always retaining its pristine beauty and sleek lines. But the texts of the plethora of safety directives were not subject to the same type of public scrutiny which modern investigative journalism would spotlight. One could almost imagine that somewhere on an artist's easel, within the dark and secret attic of an airline office building, lay a contrasting portrait of a Viscount which had a hideous tale to tell.

No part of the rear pressure bulkhead was recovered at the site of the main wreckage, or seen by divers. Among the various pieces of debris which have been carried ashore by the tides down the years, none belonged to that localised area of EI-AOM. Like the adjacent tailplanes, the entire bulkhead is still missing after three decades. In the list of suspects for the initial causal damage to the left tailplane, as set out within the final conclusions of the 2002 study, failure of the rear pressure bulkhead is described as extremely remote. In the absence of any conclusive item of wreckage from the aft section of the airframe that judgement seems appropriate.

17

The Unthinkable

In November 2000 the Exp'Air team travelled to Ireland to pursue their detailed reconstruction of the track of EI-AOM. They first interviewed a retired engineer from Aer Lingus, a man who had been in charge of planning in 1968. On the following day they drove to my home near the village of Ashford in County Wicklow. We adjourned to the local Hunter's Hotel for a lengthy discussion on various topics which I had raised with them in memoranda. They were accompanied by Kevin Humphreys, the chief inspector at the AAIU in Dublin, who generously handed me the complete bound text of the 1999 review and a copy of the original 1970 report. I would no longer have to take the tedious path of referring to the AAIU web site for details of both reports. Humphreys and Liddy's detailed study of the files from 1970 had shown the errors in the maintenance plan operated by Aer Lingus and other areas of concern, revelations which had spearheaded the call by concerned relatives of the victims for the fresh, impartial inquiry by Exp'Air.

Yves and Manuel expressed thanks for the new items of wreckage I had uncovered in County Wexford, and they pointed me in the direction of new research

avenues which were now beginning to assume importance in their deliberations. They required greater details
of the flight patterns of migratory bird flocks, especially
in the wetland regions of Cork and Waterford. They also
requested extra local information on a report they had
received about the recovery of a wing section from a U16
Meteor target drone, supposed to have been trawled up
by a fishing vessel near the Saltee Islands in 1972. It was
alleged by the informant that the conclusions which
flowed from official study of the find had been kept
secret.

During the following week I checked out the rumour
about the Meteor wing wreckage. Eventually I was able
to determine, through the good offices of Sergeant Kevin
Edmonds at Crosshaven Garda station, that the report
was just a red herring. I did establish that a different
piece of unidentified wreckage had been handed in to
the police at Crosshaven *circa* 1994, but that item had
been transported by courier to the appropriate aviation
authority. Suzanne Crosbie of the *Cork Echo* searched the
microfilm archives for me, but there was no report of
any find by a trawler near the Saltees in the 1970s. This
was confirmed by Dan Buckley, the newspaper's
features editor, and by his colleague Liam Moore. Both
of these journalists assured me that such a discovery,
only four years after the crash, would have been front-
page news if it were true.

The Meteor incident was further evidence of the way
in which canards and innuendo still pervaded public
perceptions. These beliefs were held not only at the time
of the 1970 inquiry, but continue even today. The situation is not helped by the existence of Internet sites
which keep these rumours simmering with allegations
of a cover-up. Some contributors to those web sites quote
second-hand reports which have no basis in fact, and
which lack any hard evidence. It was almost as though

they yearn for the discovery of an incriminating severed wing of a Meteor, and the wish becomes a father to the rumour mill.

None the less, I felt some sympathy for those who continued to subscribe to conspiracy theories, and for the frustrated relatives of the sixty-one persons who had died. There were just so many believable witnesses who had described a plethora of sightings which could not be reconciled with the official findings in 1970. The authors of that report had been forced to reject the evidence of those who described a disabled aircraft as it flew a faltering path at low altitude in the skies above south-east Ireland for half an hour. In fact, the team of investigators in 1970 had no other option. It was quite clear from the radio signals at 10.51 hours and 10.57 hours that Flight 712 was safely on course at that time. It was cruising sixty miles away to the east, approaching the coast of Wales at 17,000 feet.

Yves and Manuel continued their journey in Ireland, travelling to Rosslare and Waterford. There they interviewed five witnesses whose evidence had been rejected in 1970. The French team had avowed to start from scratch and their inquiries diligently covered old ground in addition to new avenues. Three days later they adjourned to Paris, to be joined by Colin Torkington. An assessment was made of the implications of the growing discrepancy between the track as seen by many observers and the route described in the conclusions within the 1970 report. A decision was made to travel again to Ireland at the end of November to interview further witnesses. In addition, they were now anxious to speak to two Air Traffic Control personnel, the Shannon supervisor and the Shannon controller, both of whom had been on duty on the morning of 24 March 1968. They were interviewed, but could shed no light on the anomalies which were becoming obvious. Yet, despite the assurances of the Shannon personnel, the pains-taking reconstruction of the flight path continued to remain at variance with the radio signals from the crew of the Viscount.

An unthinkable possibility now began to slowly edge its way towards centre stage.

18

The Splash

It was an inconclusive observation in the 1970 report, but for some reason it began to intrigue me. A witness located near Carnsore Point affirmed that he had seen a splash in the sea at about 11.00 hours GMT. Something had appeared to impact the water surface close to the Saltee Islands. The splash site was a considerable distance from the crash location near Tuskar Rock, where the aircraft wreckage was finally discovered three months later. Several independent observers in diverse locations made statements to the effect that they had seen a silver-coloured object which continued to float in the locality of the Great Saltee Island for some hours. As it rose on the crest of successive waves, some people described it as a wing-like structure. The authors of the 1970 report had used these sightings to support the hypothesis that an unmanned aircraft may have fallen into the sea there, adding fuel to the theory that EI-AOM had collided with a target drone or guided missile.

The rate-of-climb idiosyncrasy on my graph kept haunting me. I tried to mentally visualise a set of circumstances aboard EI-AOM which might fit in with the described splash and floating airfoil, other than a mid-air collision. In the midst of this introspection a singular and challenging alternative began to manifest itself. What if the wing-like object was not from another airborne object at all, but from the Viscount itself?

People who have no experience at sea or in the air frequently display a lack of precision in their judgement of distant objects. The floating piece was described as a 'wing'. However, when some witnesses had been asked in 1968 about the size of the object, at least two of them gave an estimate of 'eight square feet', while another compared its area to a single sheet of galvanised roofing. These small measurements are a more accurate description of an elevator, or perhaps even a tailplane. This possibility is reinforced when coupled to the statement of a witness who had added that when the object rose briefly on each wave crest it appeared to taper at one end. Another man who observed it through field glasses was emphatic that one end of the object was oval, while the other end had an uneven edge. No less than four independent witnesses continued to observe this object, which remained afloat and awash for about three hours. One witness even photographed the mystery item, and handed the prints to the authorities. There is no mention of these photos in the 1970 report, and it has not proved possible to find any reference to them in the files which survive.

I had already stuck my neck out with the suggestion to Exp'Air about an initial problem at an early stage in the flight, perhaps from a bird strike during the climb. If that theory was to make any headway, then the next logical step should be some attempt to reconcile any unexplained sightings with it. In for a penny, in for a pound, was my frame of mind as I rattled the PC keyboard once more with another missive to France, spelling out my speculative suggestion:

No credence was given to Witness No. 20 because the splash which he reported was in a different direction, bearing south-west of the ultimate crash site.

But what if that was a tailplane or elevator from EI-AOM, impacting the sea surface? Can any of the other witness statements be explained in terms of tailplanes, rather than an aircraft? We must bear in mind that these people were not necessarily familiar with any aspects of aviation, or proficient at aircraft type spotting. Nor would their ability to determine distances and headings over water be of a high standard.

The mental construction of such imagined scenarios is a risky task and must be tempered by the art of the possible and the likely. I now allowed my mind to wander along a hypothetical sequence which could follow a bird strike during the climb. If minor initial damage had led to progressive deterioration of a tail surface, there would come a time when a critical component such as a hinge, torque tube, spigot or even a spar might fail. The ensuing struggle to maintain flight, especially if high manual forces were required on the control column, would preclude radio transmissions. Such signals to distant ground stations would be of no help to the crew while they concentrated solely on the immediate task of sheer survival. Even if a signal was transmitted, it would not be read at Shannon ATC. A line of hills east of Shannon precluded signal clarity from any aircraft on the reconstructed track of EI-AOM at altitudes below 3,000 feet. Air crews were fully aware of this local knowledge. After the initial dive at 10.42, the Viscount flew at very low altitude. Users of mobile phones today often become aware of such localised 'black spots' in signal coverage. It was also likely that any excessive manoeuvre could readily stress the airframe beyond its design limitations, leading to separation of an elevator and then a tailplane from the empennage. If that were to happen, it would provide a very credible explanation for the floating airfoil and the relatively small splash, sighted far from the immense column of water which had pinpointed the main crash area.

There was something else too. The beachcomber Martin Connolly had spotted a glinting piece of wreckage in the sands which he trod daily near Greenore Point. It was eighteen inches long and could not float. It had worked its way ashore amid a mass of seaweed. Within a few hours of its surrender to the authorities it was identified as a piece of the spring tab from EI-AOM. This pitch control aid is fitted to the trailing edge of the elevator which is hinged to the tailplane on the left side of a Viscount.

From the high ground near his home, Martin pointed out to me the exact location where he had originally found the section, which is from the inner half of the spring tab, nearest to the vertical rudder of the aircraft. If the left elevator had detached in flight, the spring tab would have remained attached for a short period before separating from it, due to distortion or failure of the hinges and pintles during the descent or impact with the sea. The spot where it was found is twelve kilometres from the site of the crash. The prevailing sea currents flow north-east and south-west on alternating tides across the sea bed at the main wreckage location. They would carry any such small piece of loose debris away from the beach where the tab section was found. The main current which feeds the tab discovery location flows around the tip of Carnsore Point and ebbs from the waters to the south. It was there, from his clear vantage point near Tacumshane Lake, that another witness had reported a 'mushroom of water out to sea' between Black Rock and Carnsore Point.

If the object which was seen floating semi-submerged for some hours off Great Saltee Island by other witnesses was indeed the left elevator, then it follows that the described mushroom of water much closer to the mainland could have been caused by another part of EI-AOM. The left and right tailplanes, and their respective elevators, were not sighted by divers who searched the main wreckage site. The only tailplane part they recovered in that location was an outer section of the trim tab from the right elevator, measuring about 39 inches long.

The slowness of the journey of the spring tab section along the sea bed indicates that it had travelled a considerable distance, aided by some relentless current. On the October morning when it finally came into view, jettisoned on the high tide and enfolded in seaweed, six months had elapsed since the crash date.

19

The Casa Clone

If you had glanced skyward just north of Waterford on 21 June 2001, you might well have stopped breathing for a moment or two. The steady sounds from the two turboprop engines on the Casa aircraft of the IAC went suddenly silent, and she rolled into a steep descending right-hand turn. As the radius of the corkscrew tightened in answer to increasing back pressure on the control column, the aircraft continued its frightening spiral path to earth. At low altitude, the recovery by the pilot brought the aeroplane back to straight and level flight, and it climbed once more to safety.

A few miles away near Tory Hill, an observer in his mid-forties watched the unusual manoeuvres of the Casa with intense concentration. Long ago on a Sunday morning in March 1968 he had stood in the very same spot which he now occupied, feeding cattle in the field. This time he was not alone, and the men with the serious faces who accompanied him joined in the observations, stopping briefly to jot short notes on their pads. If these French aviation experts should fail to shed some light on the riddle of Flight 712, then it would not be for want of trying imaginative paths of investigation, bordering on the audacious.

As the year 2000 had drawn to a close, there had begun a series of events which would soon rock the very foundations of the original 1970 report. One fervent hope for the French inquiry was an expectation that it might finally disprove the theory of a missile strike and this was eventually achieved. But there was a price to pay for the success of the intense scrutiny which led to this riddance.

The professionalism of aircrew working up at the sharp end of any airliner is matched only by the men and women in Air Traffic Control, equally cognisant of their heavy responsibilities. There are formal procedures in place for the language they use and for the method of address, to avoid the dangers of ambiguity. If background static noise exists, or a signal is weak, this caution extends to such practices as citing the figure five as 'fife', while nine is denoted by 'niner'. In their normal spoken form these two figures have a similar acoustic tone and can be confused when signal clarity is poor. For example, a disastrous collision can occur if two aircraft are cleared to Flight Level One Five Zero, when it was intended that one of them should be at Flight Level One Nine Zero. A certain degree of informality is tolerated, but the basic safety procedures are never ignored.

The first word in any properly structured radio transmission from a ground station is the call sign of the receiving aircraft. It is essential that the crew know with certainty that a signal refers to their flight and to no other. As a secondary check, the receiving aircraft repeats its call sign when it replies. Yet some calls from Shannon to EI-AOM were not prefaced by that aircraft's call sign, an informal practice which would border on acceptability if Flight 712 was the only airborne station on the working radio frequency. The mystery lay in the fact that there were two other aircraft, EI-112 and G-APMC, sharing the ether with Flight 712 at the time of 10.41 hours.

These aircraft did not vacate the frequency until some time later, with the last one leaving at 10.47 hours. So how did the crew of EI-AOM know that the transmissions from Shannon were directed to them? Now every transcribed radio call was being viewed as though by the uneasy curator of an art gallery who gets a sudden notion that a Rembrandt, which hangs in pride of place, is not all that it seems to be.

At 10.39 plus 45 seconds, EI-AOM switched from Cork Approach radio frequency, and made its first contact with Shannon Area Control. The crew reported their position, altitude, and the time estimate for arrival at Tuskar: 'By Youghal, passing through 75, climbing to 170, Tuskar 57.' Why, then, did the controller call a mere ninety seconds later, requesting their altitude: 'Your present level?' This latter question was not prefaced by the call sign '712' at a time when the two other aircraft were maintaining a listening watch on the frequency. But the crew of Flight 712 *did* know that the request was intended for them, because they responded instantly: '712 is passing 90.' This indicates that the real time of the latter signal was not 10.41 hours, but after 10.47 hours, when EI-AOM was the sole aeroplane under control by Shannon.

The French team had access to additional research aids, such as the relevant progress strips from the air traffic controllers' desks, and the actual logs in use on the day. Yves and Manuel were now exploring reports by some new witnesses who had answered a public call to come forward. They were also revisiting the statements made to police in 1968 by those who were located west of Waterford. These latter documents had lain undisturbed in the old files for thirty-three years. The dusty files had been handed to Exp'Air by the Irish authorities. The 1970 investigators had naturally based their findings on the validity of the radio tapes, but they had been unable to reconcile the contents of the statements made by many witnesses with the transcripts. Instead, these sightings were deemed to relate either to later search aircraft or to some mysterious unmanned machine. Yet it required a quantum leap in denial to ignore the fact that some of the rejected witnesses had referred to a large four-engine plane, while others described the green and silver livery of an Aer Lingus aircraft.

The team at Exp'Air now embarked on an imaginative step. They set about reconstructing the track based solely on the evidence of witnesses, to see what the result would be if the radio transcripts were ignored. Piece by piece the bits of the jigsaw started to click into place, and the evidence from every observer verified each other's statements. A startling picture began to emerge, which was at variance with all previously held tenets. The reconstruction clearly showed that Flight 712 never reached her allocated cruise altitude of 17,000 feet, but had sustained an initial upset at an altitude close to 9,000 feet above Old Parish in County Waterford at about 10.42 hours. This discovery presented a major difficulty for Exp'Air, and continues to pose problems today. According to the Shannon radio transcripts EI-AOM had transmitted from her cruise level not just once, but on two occasions. These calls came just before 10.52 hours and again at 10.57 hours, one minute before the distress call.

The AAIU successfully traced the present whereabouts of a linchpin witness who was about thirteen years old in 1968. His evidence concerned the last missing sector of the flight reconstruction and he dutifully agreed to take part in an experiment. With the co-operation of the IAC, the Casa aircraft, normally used for maritime surveillance duties, was flown along the newly reconstructed track. The IAC crew had been briefed on the happenings which the witness had seen in 1968, and they set about reproducing the events. The visibility on 21 June 2001 was not as good as on the crash date, and the demonstration machine was a smaller aircraft than a Viscount. Despite these handicaps, the details of the observer's statement were readily verified by his ease of sighting of the Casa flight patterns, and confirmed in the presence of the Exp'Air team.

The appalling vista could no longer be shelved. The witnesses may have been right all the time. Was it possible that there were errors in the certified radio transcripts?

20

The Haughey
Connection

The texts of various interdepartmental memoranda between government ministers at the time of the crash are now available for public scrutiny. They reveal a sordid and shameful scenario of penny-pinching, and a puzzling lack of zeal to find the cause of the accident. The real reason why so much wreckage still lies on the sea bed, perhaps even including the vital missing tailplanes, was slowly dawning on me. One shining exception within this depressing correspondence raised my spirits.

He seems to have been a very decent fellow, that Brian Lenihan. He was Minister for Transport and Power at the time. You can tell a lot about a man when you have access to his personal letters, written within the ponderous and secret wheels of government in 1969. My personal political views have always leaned towards socialism, forged from friendships with maritime crews who were constantly exploited by greedy shipowners, and reinforced by my contacts with the aboriginal people of Australia. But Lenihan appears to have been the type of honourable and upright politician who, although his world most likely veered to the right of centre, could quite easily have tempted people of my left-leaning ilk to cross the line and vote for him.

A question which constantly arises concerning the Tuskar accident relates to the missing tailplanes. There are some strong indicators that the solution to the crash may lie with one or both of them, wherever they are. These are the two horizontal surfaces which extend outwards on each side of a plane's tail, below the vertical fin and rudder. In the US they are called stabilisers, for a very good reason. In simple terms, their function is similar to the effect of human hands gripping the ends of the shafts on a two-wheeled cart, which is being pushed ahead. If you let go of the shafts, or if they snap, the cart will tip to an unstable attitude. Instead of hands, the force on a tailplane is exerted by the airflow which passes above and below it. This keeps the main wings at the correct angle to the airflow, using the long fuselage as a lever. Hinged surfaces, called elevators, extend behind the tailplanes, and these are angled up or down by pulling or pushing the pilot's control column to climb or descend, combined with appropriate changes in engine power. Unlike the main wings, which give lift, the tailplanes exert leverage downward.

By July 1969 much wreckage had already been recovered by the heavy lifting equipment aboard the British naval vessels which had been contracted to assist. But there was still no sign of the critical tailplanes or elevators, apart from two small tab pieces. It became increasingly important to discover if the elevators, with their attendant spring and trim tabs, were secure on the tailplanes, one or both of which may have sustained failure or damage, or had detached prior to the final minutes. Equally important was the fact that the vertical tail fin and rudder, together with one of the four propellers, were still missing. Failure of any one of these components could have initiated the fatal spin.

Yves Lemercier (left) and Manuel Pech, members of the international team that investigated the crash, pictured at a press conference after the report was published. (Courtesy of Irish Examiner*)*

Colin Torkington, the Australian member of the International Team (left), pictured with Mary O'Rourke, Minister for Public Enterprise, and Yves Lemercier. (Courtesy of Irish Examiner*)*

Tuskar Rock, located about six miles off the Wexford coast. Its name is forever associated with the loss of EI-AOM. The aircraft struck the sea in the background, 1.7 nautical miles distant. About 65 per cent of the wreck was raised before shifting sands covered it. The remainder lies at a depth of 234 feet. (Courtesy of John Eagle Photography)

Recovered wreckage of the Aer Lingus Viscount. (Courtesy of Irish Examiner*)*

Recovery of one of the four Rolls-Royce DART turboprop engines. (Courtesy of Irish Examiner*)*

One of the four propellers from the ill-fated Viscount, brought ashore at Rosslare on 23 July 1968. The last missing propeller was skilfully retrieved from the seabed by trawler skipper Billy Bates during a renewed search in August 1969. (Courtesy of Irish Examiner)

Hook Lighthouse. (Courtesy of Keewi Photography)

Nose of an American Airlines plane on the ground at Charles de Gaulle airport, Paris. The effects of bird strikes are clearly visible.

Sir Peter Scott by the window of his studio in Slimbridge. (Courtesy of Lady Philippa Scott)

Bewick's Swan. (Courtesy of Lady Philippa Scott)

Captain O'Beirne with his son, David, who wrote the Foreword to the book. David was 21 months old when his father died. (Courtesy of Bega O'Beirne, widow of the commander of Flight 712)

Very recent photo of David O'Beirne.

Captain O'Beirne having a cup of tea, a smoke of his pipe, and a chat with his wife before heading to Dublin Airport to take command of a flight. (Courtesy of Bega O'Beirne, widow of the commander of Flight 712)

On St Patrick's Day 1968, Paul Heffernan, co-pilot of Flight 712, flew to London to act as godfather to his newborn nephew Peter. The infant was the first son of his brother Des. Paul stood over six feet tall, and is seen sporting a shamrock on his raincoat. This photo is treasured by his five siblings. On the following Sunday he died, aged 22. (Courtesy of Des Heffernan, brother of the co-pilot)

The beachcomber Martin Connolly (Witness No. 17 – 1970 Report), who helped the author to retrieve a dozen wreckage items kept by souvenir hunters in 1968.

Section of wreckage from EI-AOM, recovered by the author at Greenore Point in October 2000. A visible crack was stopped by a rivet hole or by a drilling designed to arrest such propagation. The crack may have resulted from the crash impact forces or from airframe stresses during the dive recoveries. All the rivets, with 15 mm centres spacing, pulled through.

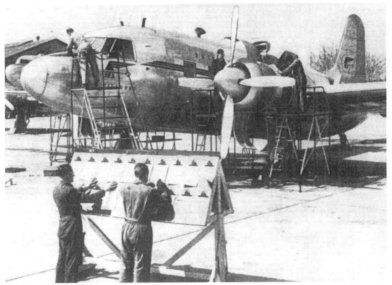

This photograph shows clearly the methods then current to keep track of the regulatory compliance periods between checks. The paper records of the '2.04' Inspection of EI-AOM, scheduled for 18 December 1967, were found to be missing when the annual Certificate of Airworthiness fell due for renewal on 6 February 1968. Despite this, the certificate was issued, 46 days before the crash. Apart from a single Job Card (No. 15), the records remain missing to this day. (Courtesy of Odhams Press Ltd)

Section of the tail fin and rudder of EI-AOM, recovered by local trawler skipper, Billy Bates. (Courtesy of AAIU website)

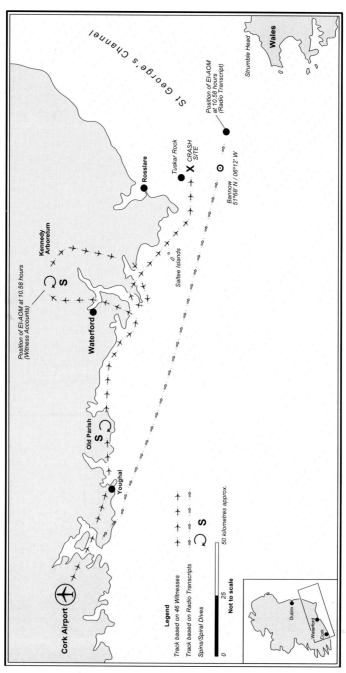

The contrasting Flight Paths. The upper track is verified by 46 independent witnesses. The lower track is the path which is based on the transcripts of the radio signals exchanged between EI-AOM and the ground stations.

Viscount EI-AOM, the aircraft which crashed near Tuskar Rock. It is pictured in its KLM livery shortly before it was sold to Aer Lingus. Its Dutch registration was PH-VIG. (Courtesy of Günter Grondstein)

Viscount EI-AOF, which crashed on 22 June 1967 on a training flight above County Meath, killing the three pilots aboard. It is pictured in its Aer Lingus livery, exactly as its sister ship EI-AOM appeared when it took off from Cork on its final and fatal flight. Similarities in the two crashes, which occurred within nine months of each other, caused the international study team to suggest that it would now be of interest to re-open the file on EI-AOF, following the 2002 conclusions on the Tuskar Rock crash. (Courtesy of Günter Grondstein)

It is obvious from the interdepartmental memoranda that Lenihan had a good grasp of the importance of a renewed search. Although the British ships had ceased searching on 21 August 1968, a reduced hunt by trawlers continued until 5 October, when the allocated funds ran out. Lenihan was told that Billy Bates, then skipper of the trawler *Glendalough*, was the man who had first pin-pointed the crash site, and that he had a comprehensive knowledge of the sea bed and tidal currents in the area of the Tuskar Rock. It would require only a very modest sum to mount a renewed search using a chartered trawler. On 10 July 1969 Lenihan sent a memo to Charles Haughey, Minister for Finance, with a routine request to approve a puny sum 'not exceeding £2,000'. The reply from Haughey on 18 July rejected the request. Lenihan was devastated.

The Minister for Finance now arrogantly assumed the mantle of salvage specialist, firm in his assessment that all reasonable steps were complete. Later events would show that whatever he knew about money, he knew nothing of the skills of Billy Bates, a man who was acquainted with the sea bed in that region as intimately as with his kitchen floor. Haughey replied to Lenihan:

> In the Minister's opinion all reasonable measures have already been taken and public funds should not be committed to any further expenditure particularly since the sum of £2,000 mentioned might well have to be considerably exceeded under pressure if public interest, now dormant, were resuscitated. The Minister regrets accordingly to be unable to sanction the proposal.

It was a shabby and ignoble response. At stake was a timescale which was now fast running out. The bulk of the remaining debris still lay at the edge of the shallow depression on the sandy bottom 234 feet below the surface. It was 1.7 nautical miles from Tuskar Rock, with the lighthouse bearing 280 degrees from the crash site. Soon the area would become silted over by the currents which often run at 6 knots near the sea bed there, shifting the sands as they flow. If any bits of wreckage could be trawled up now, they might help to eliminate, or confirm, some possible cause of a disaster which had cost sixty-one lives. All that was needed was a small but adequate sum to compensate Billy Bates for loss of his fishing income during the period of a renewed search.

The resolute Lenihan must have been appalled, evidenced by the fact that he dug in his heels and fought back. On 22 July 1969 he wrote again to Haughey at length, confessing that he was now also in discussions with Aer Lingus about concerns that any extended search for the truth by trawling operations might give rise to further damaging publicity. In that financial year the company was facing a loss of £300,000.

It is of great credit to Brian Lenihan that he resisted both Haughey and those pundits whose only horizon was profit and loss. He could quite easily have taken the politically expedient course of action, and capitulated. Instead, he announced that any unfavourable publicity 'would not, and should not in any case, be allowed to outweigh the overriding considerations of safety and the public interest'. Simultaneously he lectured Haughey on where their joint public duties lay. In a thinly veiled threat to the Minister for Finance, Lenihan informed him that 'any decision to refuse the insignificant funding on financial grounds alone would be completely indefensible if it ever became public.'

He was now so angry that he upped the ante by lobbying on behalf of the Inspector of Accidents to the effect that the trawling, 'if initially successful, should be continued for as long as useful material is being recovered'. He had laid down his marker, and if the renewed search expenditure was to exceed £2,000, then so be it. His adamant stance yielded results. On the last day of July 1969 Haughey grudgingly approved the small sum required. The hunt was on again.

Early on an August morning in 1969, the trawler *Thomas McDonagh* put to sea from her berth at Kilmore Quay. Billy Bates was in command as he headed for the crash site. During that month, and the September which followed, he successfully recovered a considerable number of valuable wreckage items from the deep. At his disposal was only the simplest of retrieval tools, a trawl net, which lacks the sophistication and technology of purpose-built salvage vessels. With great skill and seamanship he gingerly lifted an enormous entire section of the vertical tail fin, with its rudder attached. Now the investigators could be sure that those parts were in place at impact and they were eliminated as a cause of the tragedy. Only three of the four propellers had been recovered earlier, but now Bates used his deftness to capture the last one in the trawl. It immediately became clear that all four engines and propellers had been intact, and it was possible to deduce that at the last moment the handling pilot had selected flight fine pitch on the propeller blades to create maximum drag, in an attempt to lessen the imminent crash forces. As each day passed, Bates continued to strike gold. Next to break the surface was some baggage, followed by a part of the starboard main spar boom, radio racks, fuselage skin pieces, the nose-wheel bracing structure, and sections of flap and of the rudder trim tab.

Astonishingly — it was now eighteen months after the crash — it appears that only the smallest pieces of wreckage had become covered by sand movements. From this it may be deduced that if a continuous all-out effort with a realistic budget had been made in the immediate months following the location of the wreck, then the outcome could have been very different and the cause of the crash might have been quickly determined. The rumours and innuendo which still prevail are clearly shown to be nonsensical paranoia, if a study is made of the then-secret UK report on the search and salvage. Within that report, under the section marked 'General Observations and Conclusions', lies a telling summary of the real problems faced by their salvage ships:

> It was unfortunate that the operation was curtailed when it was. From the start it was difficult to plan a progressive salvage operation. On arrival at Tuskar on 20 May, I was told by the Chief of Irish Naval Staff that if the aircraft was not found in this phase, his Government would call it off. When the aircraft was found we were given one chance to raise it. This attitude prevailed throughout the operation, each visit was the last. Trying to work under these terms, in addition to the general difficulties encountered in an operation of this nature, had its effect on all concerned. The general feeling was always trying to grab what we could, in case we were not coming back. I feel this is no way to run a major salvage task.

It is a great irony that, some three decades later, Mr Haughey would be called before a public tribunal of inquiry to answer questions, among other allegations, of a diversion of funds, collected to defray expenses created by a lifesaving liver transplant operation on Lenihan. Haughey has vehemently denied that there is any substance in the suggestions, and to judge by the high standards of service to duty exhibited by Lenihan in 1969, it is probably fair to say that he, too, would be aghast at any such allegations. Even when allowing for inflation trends, the sums involved in the recent tribunals touching on Haughey are many multiples of the £2,000 which Lenihan had so much difficulty in extracting from the erstwhile Minister for Finance all those years earlier to further the pursuit of the truth about the crashed Viscount.

Perhaps even more ironic is the fact that another minister, who dutifully agreed in 2000 to initiate the new French inquiry into the crash of EI-AOM, placing it outside Ireland to ensure independence of its functions, was a woman named Mary O'Rourke. In a serendipitous twist of fate she is a sister of the late Brian Lenihan.

21

Below Zero

About a week after I had first raised the issue of icing with Exp'Air, I stumbled across some startling data, a more recent appraisal within the US of the implications for world fleets created by the loss of control in a turboprop aircraft above Indiana in 1994.

Sometimes a less experienced piston pilot like myself can get confused by the minutiae of a hitherto unknown design problem, which suddenly manifests itself in a fleet of popular workhorse air transports. Perhaps it was naive of me to assume that the standards required for passenger certification of a particular aeroplane type would filter out such defects before it went into service. I was aware of some instances in aviation history where the designers had failed to anticipate such a flaw. At the time of the Comet disasters in the 1950s, nothing was known of the cumulative effects of hull pressurisation cycles on riveted fuselages. The Lockheed Electra design had suffered failure of a wing spar, caused by torsion flexing forces exerted by the engines. In more recent years, the Douglas DC-10 type crashed when a vulnerable closure latch caused the cargo door to fail and the cabin floor to collapse, fouling the control runs to the tail. Even the ubiquitous Boeing 737 is under suspicion because of rudder reversal problems in the hydraulic control, which led to two fatal crashes. Many Boeing types have to ensure that fuel tank contents do not fall below certain levels, since an electric pump within the tank can detonate an explosive mix of vapour. But I could not understand why, with the ability to simulate so many permutations of airflow contours and other environmental conditions in a wind tunnel, the defect which existed in the wing of the ATR-72 was not spotted. It was a threat far greater than the chilled 'O-ring', which caused the Challenger space shuttle disaster. That vehicle was exploring space, with known risks. The other was transporting innocent crews and their trusting fare-paying passengers.

In fairness to the authors of the 1970 report, it should be stated at once that the recently discovered sinister aspects of airframe icing were not known in that era. The new data was gleaned by US investigators who were charged with the task of solving a very puzzling crash. The FDR, recovered at the crash site, revealed an unusual and sudden roll of the aircraft, which led to an immediate loss of control. All on board the turboprop perished. The factor which caused me to focus on the fresh revelations was the exclusive emphasis laid by the FAA on aircraft with turboprop engines. Perhaps their special vulnerability may lie in the fact that they are more frequently used on shorter hauls and at lower altitudes, where they are exposed to icing conditions with greater frequency than jets. I was unable to ignore the fact that EI-AOM was a Viscount, the world's first turboprop airliner.

On 31 October 1994 the ATR-72 in question, a joint Italian and French design and operated by American Eagle, was delayed in a holding pattern above Indiana while awaiting landing clearance. The plane continued to orbit within freezing drizzle and began to accumulate a ridge of ice just behind the de-ice boots on the leading edges of the wings. These boots are a rubber compound surface, which expands and contracts to crack any accumulated ice, causing it to detach. In this instance, too little ice built up on the boots to burden the anti-ice system and the crew was denied any warning that their aircraft was in peril. If they had been remotely aware of the fatal build-up, they would have departed from the icing conditions. Instead, the ice ridge behind the boots continued relentlessly to extend rearward. On the ATR-72 type, the wings are located quite far back on the fuselage, and impossible to view from the cockpit. The aerodynamic qualities of the wing began to degrade and a phenomenon called 'unexpected aileron hinge moment reversal' occurred. At the time of the upset the aircraft was on autopilot, which was unable to cope with the deteriorating performance of the wing. This led to a sudden roll excursion, with tragic results.

It seemed to me that a more emphatic look should now be made at the possible, albeit unlikely, chance that EI-AOM had accumulated some ice during the climb phase between 6,000 feet and 13,000 feet, where 'moderate' icing was after-cast. During the early weeks of my research and correspondence with Exp'Air, I had studied in detail the records of Viscount icing accidents. At least three of these related to a tail stall, arising from an interruption of the airflow at the tailplane/elevator hinge line, and caused by a build-up of ice. In some other fatal and unexplained Viscount crashes, ice was also on the list of suspects. As horizontal stabilisers on the tail of an aircraft, tailplanes balance the tendency of the nose to pitch down by downward airflow forces exerted on their inverted airfoils. An aircraft tail has a smaller leading edge radius and chord length than the wings, which leads it to accumulate up to three times more ice than the wings, proportional to the areas, on an unseen part of the airframe. When tail stall occurs, its downward force diminishes, or is removed entirely, causing the nose to pitch down.

At this juncture the human factors come into play. Recovery from a tail stall requires the pilot to make control inputs which are the exact opposite of those required for the more usual recovery from a stalled wing. In the latter instance it is essential to immediately reduce the angle of attack of the wings by forward pressure on the control column, which increases the airflow passing the upper wing surface. In a tail stall it is necessary to restore the airflow to the *lower* surface of the tailplane airfoil. This requires the pilot to fight his or her natural instincts and pull backwards on the control column. On some aircraft types the force required to accomplish this remedial action may call for the exertions of both pilots. They must now also resist the temptation for any power increase to gain extra airspeed, unless a wing stall is imminent. It is quite a juggling act.

It was a depressing exercise to search the archives for evidence that the Viscount design was vulnerable to ice accretion. It was necessary to be thorough with my efforts but each new discovery brought me no cheer, and I lamented the awful death toll as I added to the list.

N242V was operated by Continental Air Lines and all on board had died when she crashed at Kansas City on 29 January 1963. In the remarkably short period of time required to descend on her final approach, the Viscount flew through local icing conditions. In that brief span, the dihedral tailplanes accumulated enough rime ice to cause total loss of pitch control. Viscount SE-FOZ was also making a descent for only a limited time when she, too, picked up ice, diving into a car park at Kalvesta in Sweden from 1,150 feet. The investigators stated that 'Ice on the leading edge of the stabiliser resulted in flow separation and stabiliser stall.' There were no survivors.

In a mysterious fatal accident to a Viscount operated by Icelandair, the pilot lost control of TF-ISU near Nesoy Island, off the coast of Norway. Once again, ice on the stabiliser was believed to be a possible cause. On that day, 14 April 1963, a mere two months had elapsed since the ice accident to N242V. I had a look at older US files and spotted a Capital Airlines crash which had occurred at Freeland on 6 April 1958. This disaster had occurred not long after the introduction of Viscounts and the aircraft N7437 had logged very few hours. Yet there was a weary similarity in the official findings, which stated that the aircraft had stalled, followed by an over-the-top spin. The subsequent plunge, which killed all forty-seven persons on board, was attributed to 'an undetected accretion of ice on the horizontal stabiliser which, in conjunction with specific airspeed and aircraft configuration, caused a loss of pitch control'.

I was almost certain that the aerodynamic experts in France would be aware of the implications arising from the ATR-72 crash, and I limited myself to a preamble, followed by some details about the accident, knowing that the hint might remind them to consider the vague possibility that icing could have been a factor in the loss of an Irish turboprop.

I discovered later that Yves had in fact acted as the accredited representative of the Bureau Enquétes-Accidents to the NTSB during the 1994 investigation into the ATR-72 icing crash. I had been trying to teach my grandmother how to suck eggs.

22

A Sign from Heaven

Research can be a wearying process. Sometimes weeks may pass when no headway is made and the focus on a hypothesis is in danger of becoming lost. I found myself in an occasional dead end, based on some theory with shaky foundations. Enthusiasm becomes blunted, and each sunset at the end of another abortive day only adds to the growing lethargy. The new year of 2001 began in a spirit of optimism, as I set about fine-tuning fresh data which I had garnered from various sources.

Within a few weeks, the tracks of the Bewick's swans and the Whooper swans were firmly established. Their migratory routes and likely altitudes put them on a potential collision course with the track of EI-AOM. It was suspected that something had initiated lethal damage to the tail area of the Viscount. It could have resulted from corrosion, propagation of a fatigue crack, or even tab flutter. But equally a collision with an individual bird or a flock could have started the process of degradation. The latter theory remained in the realm of speculation. I yearned for a specific example to present to the French team — a European strike which had happened during the migratory months of March and April. I could not immediately find one in the records available to me, but

I consoled myself with the thought that some may have occurred before the advent of computer databases. It was also possible that pilot reports of non-fatal incidents and close shaves are not retained on file indefinitely.

I learned with interest in January 2001 that a Ryanair Boeing 737 had recently made an emergency landing at Cardiff with a damaged windscreen. At this time of the year some stragglers among the wintering flocks were still arriving. There were early media reports that it was a bird strike, but the causal factor proved to be a crack which had propagated from a blister on the heating element within the glass. As February 2001 drew to a close I was almost on the point of abandoning my search for a suitable comparative bird-strike incident. To be of maximum significance it had to have occurred near the end of March or early in April, and where Irish birds could have been involved. On 8 March 2001 an overseas bird strike was reported. A Bell 206 helicopter was approaching the helipad at Barnes-Jewish Hospital in Missouri, transporting a heart patient. During the final approach at 500 feet, a mallard duck crashed through the windshield, landing in the lap of the unfortunate startled patient. The pilot was partially incapacitated and suffered slight injuries but he managed to put the aircraft down safely. Although the helicopter episode was of passing interest, I kept watching for news of a relevant European strike to a much bigger fixed-wing machine, and at a higher altitude.

And then it came. It happened on 2 April 2001, just as my frustration was bordering on a mild depression. Not only did it meet all the criteria but in an astonishing eerie fortuity the big wide-body jet literally rattled the roof tiles of Manuel's office near Paris, as the crew struggled back to Charles de Gaulle Airport on one engine. I saw it as a sign from heaven, and I immediately searched for any available details.

The west and south-west counties of Ireland are wonderful winter refuges for many breeds of birds. Among the flocks are included the northern shoveler, mallard and widgeon. These varieties of duck occur in great numbers, with the widgeon reaching an average concentration of 7,500 birds each year in Kerry alone. Widgeons in the Shannon estuary number in excess of 4,000. Having accumulated winter fat reserves, they respond to the breeding urge each March and April, heading eastwards towards Europe. The northern shoveler has major breeding grounds in Hungary. At dawn on 2 April 2001 many such birds from diverse locations continued the ongoing daily departures. A safe passage by the shovelers and other ducks was negotiated through southern Irish skies above the counties of Cork and Waterford. There was no report of a strike to any aircraft in that region, or any near-miss. As the flocks continued their climb above 10,000 feet they used the distant promontory of Land's End, to the left of their track, to orient a heading which would enable them to intercept the next navigational headland of Cap de la Hague on the French coast. Above this waypoint, they made a slight adjustment to their course. Now tracking 095 degrees towards Hungary, they joined up with flocks heading to Poland and other regions in the skies above France.

At this same time an American Airlines Boeing 767 rolled down the runway at Charles de Gaulle and began her climb to cruise altitude. N376AN was westward bound for Miami. Her passengers undid their seat belts as the outer suburbs of Paris slipped away below them. Unknown to these travellers, they would never reach cruise level. Some miles ahead, a flock of northern shovelers headed towards the jet on a collision course, unaware of the danger as they dutifully answered Nature's call to mate and breed. The gap closed as the

Boeing climbed through 14,000 feet and the flock struck the aircraft like a salvo of artillery shells. The leading bird exploded into the flight deck near the captain's left leg, causing a hole in the pressure hull through the P1-1 panel. Instant depressurisation of the aircraft followed. As the oxygen masks deployed automatically in the passenger cabin, the startled commander reached for his own life-sustaining supply. He was just about to assess the damage when another ten birds struck and punctured the aircraft in the tail, on the leading edges of the wings, and on the exposed belly which was angled upward in the climb. The right engine ingested other birds from the flock and the damage to its internal blades was so severe that it could no longer produce power. The crew shut it down and trimmed the rudder for single-engine flight. The captain gingerly turned his damaged jet back towards Paris for the imminent landing on one engine. With all thoughts of Miami now gone, the jittery passengers watched the threshold of the runway come into view, as Flight AA63 settled to earth in a safe return. The traumatised carcasses of some birds were retrieved from the interior of the aircraft structures, and ornithological experts identified the breed as northern shoveler. After repairs costing over one million dollars, the plane rejoined the American Airlines fleet. (The regular American Airlines Flight AA63 from Paris to Miami is not blessed with the best of statistical luck. Eight months after the bird strike by northern shovelers, the same flight was en route with 183 passengers and 14 crew on 22 December 2001, not long after the New York attack on the Twin Towers. About two hours into the flight from Paris, a passenger named Richard Reid tried to light a fuse to detonate explosives concealed in the heels of his sneakers. Although he weighed over 200 pounds and was well over 6 feet tall, he was subdued by cabin staff and other passengers as he lit the second match. He was held under restraint while the aircraft diverted to a safe emergency landing at Boston. In February 2003, Reid was jailed for life.)

I succeeded in acquiring close-up photographs of the impact sites on the aircraft. It is a sobering exercise to study them. A relatively small duck, the shovelers had inflicted gross damage to various surfaces. Just ahead of the nose wheel bay, the fuselage skin resembled the pre-served scene of a grisly murder. Large splotches of blood and viscera covered the rims of the holes. I was particularly interested in the patterns of the large holes in the leading edges of the airfoils. It was clear to see that if a similar sized bird had struck the left tailplane of EI-AOM during her climb above southern Ireland on 24 March 1968, then a gradual degradation and skin peeling could follow. This would readily reconcile with the statements from the new witnesses. Those documents were in process of examination in Le Vesinet to establish their correlation with the reconstruction of the final track of the Viscount, now under way.

As the weeks progressed, the flight paths of birds worldwide continued to come into conflict with the routes of the big jets. At Detroit on 26 April 2001 a Boeing 757 struck several snow geese while climbing, causing major damage to an engine. The exhaust gas temper-ature reached 700 degrees and smoke entered the cabin. A successful emergency landing on one engine was completed. On 8 June 2001 about ten Canada geese were ingested by an engine on an Airbus 300 as it approached Newark Airport. On the following day another Airbus 300 struck a Canada goose during the climb above Dayton. The affected engine was subsequently scrapped.

Although all fatal accidents to civilian airliners are carefully recorded, there is inadequate provision for detailed data on non-fatal incidents of bird strikes. The awful thought struck me that this might indicate a high frequency of such incidents, leading to nonchalance. I decided to try some air force archives, knowing that birds do not distinguish between military and civilian targets, and found that air forces keep excellent records.

Among dozens of military collisions which had a happier outcome, there were some strikes which showed the potential for disaster only too clearly. On 22 September 1995, all twenty-four American servicemen on board a Boeing E-3B Sentry died in a collision with a flock of Canada geese near Elmerdorf base in Alaska. This crash was followed by another fatal accident on 15 July 1996, when a Belgian Air Force Lockheed C-130 struck a flock of lapwings on its approach to Eindhoven in Holland. The 4 crew members died, and there were only 7 survivors among the 37 Dutch band musicians who were aboard.

I gathered together the various strands of information I had collected and I made my case to Exp'Air. When the official study was finally presented in Dublin on 24 January 2002, I was not surprised when I saw that a bird strike was listed as one of the three most likely causes of the initial damage to the left tailplane of EI-AOM. Some extracts from my work made up Appendix 3a of the French findings.

I suppose it must have been nigh impossible for Exp'Air to omit that cause from the list of prime suspects. After all, if you glance out through your office window in the outskirts of Paris, it is difficult to ignore the immense mass of a lacerated Boeing 767 airliner as it slides by at low altitude, cleared for a straight-in approach to an emergency landing. Manuel may have pondered on its severely pock-marked airframe, as a captain with sweaty palms nursed it towards the nearby airport. When the evening news bulletins gave details of the damage to that plane from multiple bird strikes, it is likely that Manuel, like myself, saw it as an omen. The world is a very big place and Le Vesinet is but a tiny speck on its surface.

23

The Pedestal Puzzle

Among the wreckage pieces recovered from the sea bed at the crash site was the cockpit pedestal. This is a raised section located in the space between the two pilots, and on many aircraft designs it is fitted with such items as the throttle levers, propeller pitch controls and small wheels with knurled rims to alter the trim of the aeroplane. It can often provide clues to certain control settings at the instant of a crash. The 1970 team of investigators had gleaned from the elevator trim position that the aircraft was trimmed nose-down by a considerable amount when she hit the sea surface. Because various other components have not been recovered, it is not possible to verify this deduction by using back-up sources. None the less, it seems appropriate to examine at face value the implications of this perplexing apparent trim setting.

It was possible to conclude from close examination of the wreckage that all four propellers were on the flight fine pitch stops. The four throttles were closed. In lay terms, this equates roughly to descending a steep hill in low gear in a motor car. This pitch setting, which creates maximum drag, may have been a last-ditch effort by the crew to lessen the impact forces. Whatever awful chain of circumstances had led to the loss of control, it is apparent that the pilots retained their cool thinking even as the sea rushed up to meet them in the final seconds.

The most puzzling feature was why nose-down trim was selected by them, if that deduction is accurate. In any attempt to ditch a disabled aircraft, the handling pilot will endeavour to minimise the rate of descent and to hold the machine just above stalling speed, using the lowest engine power necessary, in a nose-up attitude and with full flap applied. Yet when EI-AOM hit the sea, the flaps were fully retracted and the aircraft appeared to be trimmed to a nose-down setting. It does not seem to make sense, particularly when it is known that the crew were sufficiently aware and alert to take the creditable step of selecting an advantageous pitch on the propellers.

One of the classic textbook ditchings at sea was executed by Captain Richard Ogg, some twelve years before the Tuskar disaster. Two of his four engines failed above the Pacific Ocean at night, midway between Honolulu and San Francisco. He was unable to feather the blades on one propeller, causing considerable drag, which in turn meant that he now had insufficient fuel to make a landfall. Ogg turned his Pan American Boeing 377 Stratocruiser towards a coastguard weather ship, the *Pontchartrain*, which he circled in darkness until dawn. With superb skill he mushed the giant airliner on to the water surface, nose high and with full flap. The aircraft floated for a quarter of an hour, and every man, woman and child was rescued by small motor boats, launched from the coastguard cutter. In a similar accident on 23 September 1962 a Constellation of Flying Tiger Airlines Flight 923 ditched in the Atlantic, 500 miles west of Ireland. It was en route from the US to Germany and 48 survivors packed themselves into an inflatable raft designed for only 25 persons. They were picked up by a Swiss freighter, the *Celerina*.

In those two ditchings the crews had full control of yaw, pitch and roll. It seems likely that the crew of EI-AOM had eventually lost control in the pitch axis, which is almost invariably fatal. There have been survivors from some heroic pitch control struggles, when the crews managed partial success by using engine power variations. Such a desperate tactic is only possible, however, if the tailplanes are intact, even if there is loss of elevator and trim control. There is some doubt about the integrity of the tail area of EI-AOM in the final minutes of the flight. It remains possible that, towards the end, the crew were frantically occupied in trying to tame a porpoise, alternately verging on a stall followed by a dive. Such struggles usually end when the oscillations get slightly ahead of the crew response, and with total loss of control. Only a cruel scenario, with some semblance to the one described, could cause a sane crew to eventually engage flight fine pitch on all four propellers of an aircraft, and to close the throttles. There seems little doubt that they retained some roll control, as the aircraft struck the sea surface right way up and with the wings almost level.

I began to consider an imagined scenario wherein the pilots had been using applications of engine power to maintain pitch control. Perhaps there was some quirky combination which kept the nose up only when nose-down trim was used in conjunction with the opposite effect from the power surges. This type of permutation could possibly result from distortion of the tail surfaces during spin recovery. I was just about to send a memo to Manuel voicing these thoughts, when I recognised that it would be inappropriate to raise a matter which could only add to the busy Exp'Air workload at this very late stage in their deliberations. Thus it was that I decided to search through world accident records myself, to see if there were any similar incidents where a bizarre trim condition had existed. I typed up a schedule of my discoveries, and sent it to Le Vesinet, just in case they themselves had been questioning the trim setting, and might appreciate a look at some comparative situations. (The schedule and accompanying memo are set out in Appendix 2A.)

Of the nine specimen incidents which involved problems with trim control in the pitch axis, five had resulted in crashes which killed everybody on board.

24

Tender Loving Care

In general, the great majority of airline passengers have little interest in the technical aspects of aviation. They are mostly concerned about fare prices, punctuality, food and service, and the degree of leg-room and comfort in their seat. Such people could be excused for believing that a new version of their favourite aeroplane, stretched and modified, would be superior in every way to the earlier type. When Aer Lingus purchased nine Viscount 800 Series aircraft from KLM in 1966, it was naturally assumed that this model was an improvement in every way when compared to the tired 700 Series. What was not known at the time, even by many within the airline industry, was the fact that the second generation of this popular turboprop now had modified tailplanes which required lots of tender loving care, regular close inspections, and a rigid maintenance schedule.

As August 2001 drew to a close, and with the new French report due for release in September, I began a final summary of the various facets of research which had been completed in the previous year. I retraced my steps to see if there was any useful data which I could add. In the midst of this search I chanced upon an airworthiness directive issued in 1995, a relatively recent alert in respect of what was then an almost obsolete type, the Viscount 800 Series. The paragraph which caught my attention placed some emphasis on a fact that was entirely new to me. With the passage of time, and a close analysis of maintenance problems which had surfaced over the years in the world fleet of 445 Viscounts, a paradox existed. It was now known that the younger 800 type was more vulnerable to tailplane fatigue cracks than its predecessor. This was attributable to a design change in the newer fleet.

It is likely that the engineers at Vickers had a desire to strengthen the tailplane, which had suffered from problems on the introductory 700 type. It is an axiom that some design changes can lead to a compromise in other areas. A higher stress loading on some spar fittings, possibly to resist tail damage during penetration of turbulent air, now became part of the 800 Series. This configuration was therefore more vulnerable to fatigue cracks, which is a trait of metal under high stress. No doubt a suitable safe inspection and maintenance plan was formulated, to keep a wary eye on any potential crack propagation. While the design team would be aware of the swings-and-roundabouts loss of crack resistance, this is not the type of information which is emphasised by a sales team, pushing the advantages of the new upgraded version of the Viscount in the world aviation marketplace. There was nothing inherently dangerous in the high-stress fittings. It simply meant that inspection methods had to be of a very high standard, particularly in those areas of the tail which are difficult to access.

I was unsure whether or not the French team were aware of this anomaly and I knew that their report was possibly already printed in draft form. Despite this, I felt that I should advise them of the situation, primarily because tailplanes and maintenance were two items which were high on the inquiry agenda. Some late significance was apportioned by the French experts to this memo. The samples of fourteen tail-related airworthiness directives from 1955 onwards, which I had traced, eventually formed Appendix 3b of the final Study. Any reader who has a technical interest in such matters may view the somewhat startling litany on < www.aaiu.gov.ie > (Volume 2 — Appendices and Annexes).

The existence of various problems with the tail areas of all Vickers Viscount types caused me to reflect on a number of unexplained accidents, including EI-AOM. These aircraft, together with the much bigger Vickers Vanguard, all shared a tail design which had a distinctive trait. The horizontal stabilisers on each side of the tail are of dihedral angle. In simple terms they were not the conventional horizontal tailplanes of that era, but tilted upwards towards the tips, so that when viewed from behind the aircraft, they formed a shallow 'V' shape. There is little to be found in technical aviation literature to indicate whether or not that innovative design step created any unusual problems at the time.

Exactly one year before the Tuskar disaster, a Viscount 800 like EI-AOM also crashed into the sea. It was approaching East London in South Africa. Although no definite answer was found, the official report cites structural failure as a possibility. More conclusive, however, is the probable cause disclosed by the investigation into the crash of HK-1058, a Viscount which lost control as it descended through 7,000 feet in Colombia on 8 June 1974. In this case, the aircraft crashed over land and thus all of the debris was available for examination. The cause was 'Failure in flight of the tailplane spar, causing the left tailplane and elevator to detach.' Then, on 15 August 1976, Viscount HC-ARS disappeared while at cruise altitude, and the wreck is believed to lie somewhere in the remote regions of Ecuador. Four years later, PK-IVS crashed into a swamp near Jakarta, when a part of the tail detached in flight. That Indonesian aircraft was a Viscount 800 type and all on board were killed.

While thoughts of these accidents occupied part of my waking hours, another factor began to slowly intrude. As we have seen, substantial errors had existed in the Aer Lingus Maintenance Plan for a year before the crash of EI-AOM. It was time to ask a hard and unavoidable question. Could any one, or both, of these paperwork flaws have impinged in any way on routine inspection and maintenance of the tailplanes of the Viscount 803 fleet? We now know that those airfoils were overly sensitive to stress. The corrective sedative therapies insisted upon by the safety authorities were being prescribed in increasing variety and numbers. One such directive, which embraced the 800 Series, was issued as late as thirty-seven days before the Tuskar disaster. It referred to potential cracks in the elevator root and ribs.

The total collection of relevant Viscount airworthiness directives reads like the private library of a nervous hypochondriac. However, unlike that neurosis, the tailplane problems were not in the mind. They were very real, and they were bringing down real aeroplanes full of equally real people.

25

The Cry of Eureka

I wish I could say that it all became suddenly clear, like the day Archimedes lay meditating in his bathtub, eyeing the volume of displaced water. It would provide a suitable dramatic twist for a book of this nature. Unfortunately, life does not always imitate art. A more appropriate analogy for the electrifying discovery, for that is what it ultimately was, is the tedious research by Edison which led to a practical electric light bulb. His early efforts employed crude filaments made from threads of various natural fibres, impregnated with carbon. For a brief time, each experimental sample burned brightly within the glass vacuum tube, only to flare suddenly and die. The route to the modern tungsten wire filament was long and arduous. The 2002 study trod a similar road, with occasional glimpses of the likely truth. It took many months to shine the steady spotlight on a credible hypothesis, supported on pillars of very persuasive arguments.

The hypothesis which the team at Exp'Air were about to present to the Irish government still remains highly controversial, because it is at variance with the assertions of those who believe that they heard the two signals at 10.52 and 10.57 hours on the original tape, which is not available for comparison. Those were the radio calls which indicated that EI-AOM was cruising at 17,000 feet at the time of transmission. Despite the contentious nature of the Exp'Air conclusions, it would be unfaithful to the authors of the 1970 report, to the remit of Exp'Air, and to the public interest, if such a scenario was not even contemplated simply because it conflicted with the tenets of other persons. There is also an implied promissory note to Captain O'Beirne and Paul Heffernan, long overdue for payment.

Following intense discussions with various entities in Dublin, and a number of resultant delays in the release date, it was decided to publish the hypothesis of an erroneous transcript and to balance it by including any submissions of rebuttal from affected persons. One such rejection on behalf of a Shannon staff member was received by AAIU from Vincent Toher and Company, a firm of Cork solicitors, on 22 January 2002. In their letter, the lawyers do not refer to their client by name. The faxed rejection arrived two days before release of the French study. This controller was relatively young at the time and had not yet advanced to high ranking within the system. In any event, the rules forbade him from taking any part in the transcript preparation, as he was on duty for part of the relevant time period. In his statement to Exp'Air in 2000 he accepts that the signal transmitted at 10.52 hours was 'slightly weak', but he read it as 'Level at 170'. He was not even present at the control desk when the 10.57 call was allegedly transmitted from EI-AOM, having departed on his lunch break at 10.55. That signal was handled by the relief controller who has since died. The revised track of EI-AOM still remains incompatible with the Shannon radio transcript and no credible explanation for many other identified anomalies within it has surfaced, certainly not in the public arena. However, the new postulation is a corroborated thesis which is well supported by forty-six very credible witnesses. The decision to present it was not taken lightly. Each person must be his or her own judge of the likely truth behind the discrepancies.

For the benefit of readers who may have difficulty in grasping the nuances and implications of the conclusions in the 2002 study which concern the transcripts, it may help if they are reduced to very simple facts. It is irrelevant whether or not the reader is familiar with Air Traffic Control procedures, and aviation buffs have no real advantage. All that is required for comprehension is an ability to add or subtract a few four-digit numbers. The anomalies in the transcripts are initially difficult to spot. The 1970 investigators, and many experts since then, have read those typed documents without comment.

To lay the groundwork we must first understand why the radio tapes were so influential on the investigation procedures pursued in 1968. According to the transcript, Flight 712 reported to Shannon, at 10.51:48 hours, that it had just reached its cruise altitude of 17,000 feet and that it was flying 'level' at that height. At 10.57:07 hours the crew again confirmed that altitude. To this latter signal they added an estimate that they would reach the Welsh coastal headland of Strumble at 11.03 hours. This placed that promontory about five or six minutes away. When the distress call from EI-AOM was recorded on tape by London Airways, and intercepted by two other airliners on that radio frequency, the time was 10.58:10 hours. At 10.57:29 hours the Shannon transcript claims that EI-AOM transmitted a brief confirmation in routine laconic speech that they were now switching to the London radio frequency. This assertion forced the 1970 investigators to conclude that in that brief span of 41 seconds the Viscount suddenly lost control in sedate cruise flight, to descend in a rapid spin. In that fall it had already lost 12,000 feet of altitude when the distress call was made: 'Five thousand feet, descending, spinning rapidly.' The crew of another Aer Lingus aircraft, en route to Bristol, intercepted the signal and relayed the stated altitude to London Airways as '5,000 feet'. Later acoustic analysis of the London tape leaned more towards '12,000 feet', which also fitted in better with the assigned cruise altitude. But the Exp'Air track reconstruction in 2002 shows that it was indeed '5,000 feet' which was spoken, and perhaps the experts who had doubted the accuracy of the original relayed signal from experienced airline pilots did so at their peril. Such crews spend their working lives with radio headphones glued to their ears and become very adept at deciphering occasional weak or static-laden words.

Because of the calculated position of Flight 712 at 10.58 hours, nearing Strumble Head at 17,000 feet, it was understandable that the evidence submitted to police by many witnesses west of Waterford was ignored in 1968. Some of them were very young persons who described unusual flight manoeuvres of an aircraft at low altitude in those skies at about 10.45 hours, and above other nearby localities at intervals thereafter up to about 11.00 hours. The 1970 inquiry took the view that these witnesses must be mistaken and had probably observed later search aircraft. No criticism can be made of this assessment, because the investigators naturally relied on the certified transcripts which showed that it was impossible for the Viscount to be west of Waterford at that time. For three decades it has been assumed that the transcripts were a precise presentation of the audio tapes and not to be questioned.

All the clues to errors in the texts were in place since 1968. I have no belief in a sixth sense and yet I wrote a convoluted memo to Manuel in November 2000 under the heading '*Something* is wrong, and I can feel it in my bones.' However, I cannot claim some foresight at that time of the ultimate study conclusions. All of us who contributed in any small way to the 2002 Study enjoyed the luxury of experimenting with lateral concepts. Resources could be focused on tiny details, while the handicapped 1970 team experienced extreme difficulty in raising an extra £2,000 for so important a task as extending the search for wreckage by a chartered trawler. In addition, it should be borne in mind that such a study is not conducted within the more stringent remit of an International Civil Aviation Organization (ICAO) air crash inquiry, whose reports demand higher levels of irrefutable evidence and seldom stray into the realms of conjecture. If there had been only one apparent error within the transcripts, the case for the argument would be weak. Two errors would raise some doubts, while three or four would border on conclusiveness. By the time the intense scrutiny was completed, at least eight separate parts of the typed pages were causing concerns.

In the section that follows I have endeavoured to set out for the reader the plain person's guide to the mystery, stripped of any superfluous aviation jargon. It explains in basic terms the conclusion within the study which relates to the transcripts. But since that leaves a big question without an answer, I have also included a note of how the errors arose, which, it is important to state, simply consists of carefully measured guesswork. It does not represent any official view ever held by Exp'Air or their associates and remains only my personal hunch.

26

Untangling the Web

T he accuracy of the tapes from Cork Airport Control Tower and Cork Approach is not in question. The guidance duties of those facilities in relation to Flight 712 ceased at 10.39 hours, when EI-AOM was handed over to Shannon Area Control. The Viscount had taken off at 10.32 hours. It was relatively easy to establish from the altitude of 7,000 feet at 10.38 hours, reported to Cork, that the average rate of climb up to that time was about 1,150 feet per minute, which is compatible with the aircraft type. The surviving paperwork from the 1968 investigation process confirms that when the Shannon ATCO advised Flight 712 of the time correction to 'fifty-six and a half' (i.e. 10.56:30), the exact time on the recorder was 10.57:24, a difference of 54 seconds, and valid for the entire transcript. The first radio call from EI-AOM to Shannon at 10.39:45 hours confirmed that the Viscount was now only at 7,500 feet. Even without adding on the corrective 54 seconds, the elapsed time between 7,000 feet at 10.38 hours and 7,500 feet at 10.39:45 hours is 1 minute and 45 seconds. If the adjustment to recorder time is made, the gap increases to 2 minutes and 39 seconds. Yet the Shannon transcript shows that EI-AOM had gained a mere 500 feet *in total* within that time period. Immediately beforehand, between takeoff and 7,000 feet, she had been climbing at a realistic average of 1,150 feet *per minute*, as shown in the undoubted Cork transcript. There were some strange inconsistencies in the Shannon transcripts.

One of the chores often allocated to a co-pilot is calculation of the ETA at various points on the intended track. By regulation and tradition, the protocol demands that each pilot must monitor the actions of the other, including the precise language and content of radio signals. This mutual supervision greatly increases the safety margins. As soon as the Viscount lifted off the Cork runway at 10.32 hours, the ETA at Strumble Head became 11.07 hours, representing the standard routine flying time on that sector of the track, and consistent with the filed flight plan. At 10.36 hours, according to a transcript of the telephone line to London Airways, the Shannon controller informed his UK counterpart to expect Flight 712 at Strumble Head at 11.07 hours. London always attached great importance to such estimates, because these times were utilised to funnel aircraft towards the busy skies near Heathrow Airport, and to arrange safe traffic sequencing amid continuous arrivals and departures on the long parallel runways of 28 Right and 28 Left. In some circumstances a direct flight from Cork to Strumble Head was approved, which dispensed with the brief dog-leg via Tuskar. This reduced the distance by about four nautical miles which, on the day of the crash, would alter the ETA at Strumble Head to 11.06 hours. It was the standard practice for crews to adjust that ETA by one minute when the more favourable direct track was approved. At 10.40 hours Shannon requested EI-AOM to 'Confirm you are accepting a direct routing to Strumble.' Flight 712 replied: 'Affirmative. Estimating Strumble at 03.'

Both pilots were fastidious aviators, with a known penchant for attention to detail. They had flown the route many times and were very conversant with calculation of the Strumble ETA. The navigation aids beaming from Strumble Head VOR included a Distance Measuring Equipment (DME) facility. In other words, the estimate of 11.03 by the crew was not a haphazard guess but was calculated from the DME dial on their instrument panel which displayed the exact distance to Strumble. At 10.33 hours, one minute after takeoff, Cork Tower had informed the crew: '712 was airborne at 32.' Why, then, would EI-AOM radio a spurious estimate of 11.03 hours for the arrival at Strumble Head, one which was *four minutes faster* than the routing via Tuskar, rather than the normal advantage of *one minute*?

The growing litany of discrepancies in timings, procedures and the rate of climb continued. At 10.40 hours the controller requested EI-AOM to repeat an 'unreadable' message. One minute later the same controller then ignored the fact that he could not understand the signal transmitted in a second 'unreadable' call, and he failed to request verification. A silence of ten minutes then ensued, when no signals were exchanged. At 10.51:48 hours the crew made the verification 'Level at 170', followed at 10.57:07 hours by the signal '712 by Bannow, Level 170, estimating Strumble at 03.' In a strange exercise, involving a mote and a log of biblical proportions, the controller now vacillated between pedantry and nonchalance. He requested the crew to repeat the time at 'Bannow', which was confirmed by the pilot as '57'. Shannon replied: 'Okay. Time 56 and a half.' Having made this punctilious correction, it is extraordinary that the controller totally ignored the astonishing estimate for the ETA at Strumble. The distance from 'Bannow' to Strumble is forty-four nautical miles. For EI-AOM to reach the Welsh headland at 11.03 hours it would have to fly at a staggering ground speed of 440 knots, which is over 500 mph. This was an impossible feat for the Viscount aircraft type, which had a maximum cruising speed of 357 mph but was usually flown at about 310 mph in the cruise. The Shannon controller was acutely aware of the significance of the cruising speed of a Viscount. At 10.44 hours, during a confirmatory phone discussion with London (see transcript in Appendix 1), he informed his UK counterpart that the Viscount bound for Bristol from Dublin was cruising at 267 knots (about 308 mph) at 13,000 feet, and that it should reach Strumble at 11.07 hours. Other parts of the Shannon transcript contain further examples of incongruity and discontinuity within the sequence of signals. Readers who wish to examine these in detail can find them in Appendix 3C.

A question arises. What could have possibly led to such errors, if that is what they are? Exp'Air declared quite firmly in the 2002 study findings that they were not in the business of allocating blame and they made no attempt to engage in that type of fruitless exercise. Their task was to accommodate the reconstructed track of EI-AOM, and to shed any new light on the disaster. To achieve these aims it ultimately became necessary to question the accuracy of the radio transcripts. Any inconsistencies in those documents could have misled their predecessors in 1970, a team which had based the flight track on the radio signals exclusively.

There does exist a plausible explanation for the errors. It seems to me that the mistakes could have arisen from an unfortunate chain of circumstances. My view is only a personal one, but it does fit in with most of the known facts. Visualise the scene. The witnesses described the control struggles at low altitude from shortly after 10.40 hours onwards. True clarity of VHF radio transmissions requires line-of-sight between the aircraft antenna and the aerial of a ground station. Shannon may have been deaf to a Viscount flying low after its recovery from the abrupt descent seen above Old Parish, or the signals may have been unintelligible. Unable to return to Cork or to make a forced landing on a beach or field because of tail damage, which precluded a controlled landing approach flare-out, the frantically occupied crew possibly selected the London radio frequency after 15 minutes of disabled flight to try to make contact with any station on listening watch. At this time of 10.58 hours they were attempting to climb the distressed aircraft above the Kennedy Arboretum, as described in witness statements. The closest ground aerial to that area which could establish contact with London was located at Davidstow Moor in Cornwall. Today this airfield is unused, except by some keen microlight flyers. The aerial was 1,073 feet above sea level, an elevation which facilitated easier radio contacts by improved line-of-sight to distant aircraft. Indeed the Viscount could establish contact with Davidstow from as low as 5,000 feet. It is significant that the first call to London at 10.58:02 hours was in an unusual format, indicating that EI-AOM was already in distress and may have been in peril for some period prior to that. The final 'spinning' call was taped by London eight seconds later.

The typed record of the land line telephone conversations between London and Shannon ends suddenly at 10.44 hours, when by regulation it should have covered all communications up to the time when the full alert was called at 11.25 hours. The Shannon radio transcript also stops prematurely at 10.57:29. Consequently it is not possible to know details of the information exchanged when London advised Shannon of the intercepted distress signal from EI-AOM. When it became obvious that the Viscount had crashed, the staff at Shannon were immediately aware that a tape transcript would be required for the official inquiry. Since the distress call was received by London at 10.58 hours, Shannon would naturally assume that EI-AOM had passed into the UK control zone at 17,000 feet. They had no way of knowing that the call was transmitted above the Kennedy Arboretum in County Wexford at a lower altitude. The time of the distress call placed EI-AOM within about six minutes of the Welsh coast in normal flight.

If the interlocking statements of the forty-six witnesses are accepted, showing EI-AOM in distress at low altitude from about 10.42 hours, and thus unable to contact Shannon, then a transcript which shows any subsequent routine signals from the Viscount to Shannon after that time must be viewed with extreme caution. It is possible that when the relief controller came on duty at the desk at 10.55 hours to cover the lunchtime break of his colleague some overlap assumptions were made. With no message from EI-AOM to indicate that the progress of Flight 712 was anything but normal, he may have believed that the aircraft had reached its cruise level and was under control from London. At 10.39 hours the crew had reported to Shannon that they were by Youghal, climbing through 7,500 feet, and in a routine ascent to 17,000 feet. At 10.41 hours they reported at 9,000 feet. While strict regulations to deter any assumptions have always existed, some human factors can come into play which may have allowed for a more casual attitude by staff in the 1960s. In that decade the southern Irish skies were not crowded, and after 10.47 hours the Viscount was the only aircraft under control from Shannon. Familiarity with a regular flight which has a well-established pattern can induce complacency.

There exists a possibility that some unreadable or garbled signals were transmitted at low altitude by EI-AOM when it suffered its initial upset above Old Parish shortly after 10.40 hours. The Shannon controller may have innocently misread the indecipherable words, or he may have mentally ascribed a content to them which was appropriate for that stage of the 712 flight routine. Maybe he thought that the transmissions from the Viscount were temporarily affected by some unknown factor and that the signal clarity would improve when EI-AOM gained more altitude, and perhaps he waited for some time. Although the controller who handled the 10.52 transmission accepts that there was a level of weakness in the signal strength, it was not possible to secure a judgement from the relief controller concerning the 10.57 call, as he has died in the interim.

In 2000 there was a significant and subtle revelation made to Exp'Air by a leading member of the 1970 inquiry team, one who had listened to the original tape. In his statement he says 'The tape I heard was readable because I had a copy of the transcript made by ATC experts.' The human ear is a wonderful organ, but it is vulnerable to suggestive influences. The acoustic analysts who studied the weak and ambivalent '5,000 feet' final distress call from EI-AOM changed that figure later to '12,000 feet'. That higher altitude fitted in better with the figure of 17,000 feet, where they *thought* the aircraft was cruising. Sometimes we hear what we want to hear. The new track by Exp'Air restores the original figure of '5,000 feet'.

The Full Alert was not called by Shannon ATC until 11.25 hours, almost half an hour after the distress call. The premature ending, at 10.44 hours, of the transcript of the telephone conversations between London and Shannon, as presented to the 1970 inquiry, precludes any examination of the communications up to 11.25 hours. The latter time is the minimum duration which by regulation should have been covered, that is, up to the time of Full Alert. It would be helpful if the messages exchanged by phone just after 10.58 hours were available for scrutiny. Attempts were made by Exp'Air to secure the London transcript through the British AAIB, but this proved fruitless, as London was unable to trace the file after a lapse of three decades.

In November 2000 the retired Shannon supervisor made a statement to Exp'Air which claims that he felt London ATC had been too hasty in making a request to the Bristol-bound Aer Lingus Flight 362, instructing the crew to alter course and search the sea surface west of Strumble Head. The justification offered by the Shannon supervisor for any perceived tardiness in declaring the Full Alert relies on the transmission from EI-AOM at 10.57 hours, indicating that the flight was still normal at that time, about 40 seconds before the time it was then assumed that the initial upset to the Viscount had occurred. He also stated that at 11.10 hours London ATC advised Shannon that there was no radio contact with EI-AOM, and that three minutes later, at 11.13 hours, the London supervisor phoned to reaffirm radio silence from Flight 712. The Shannon supervisor claims that London did not mention the two signals they had received from EI-AOM at 10.58 hours to indicate that the flight was in distress and spinning seaward. It is for this reason that he says he was not aware of the true seriousness of the situation. Yet at 10.59 and 11.00 hours London ATC was already in urgent radio discussions with the captains of Aer Lingus Flight 362 and BOAC Flight 506 respectively, both of whom had intercepted the distress call. Even the transcript of the London 'intercom' speech between individual staff members clearly shows discussions from 11.01 hours onward about the 'spinning' transmission. It is difficult to understand why the London supervisor failed to mention the distress call to his responsible counterpart at Shannon during their urgent phone conversation at 11.13 hours, some fifteen minutes after the event, and simply restricted himself to notification of a lack of radio contact. By this time London had already diverted a passenger flight on a search mission, which was conducted a mere 500 feet above the sea by the crew of Aer Lingus 362. It is possible that Shannon ATC may have reacted to the emergency with shortcomings indicated by Exp'Air in Section 6.2.5 of their conclusions:

> The procedures which were applied in Shannon ATC at the time of the accident were either not well adapted (in particular for specific period of a transition between routine and emergency) or not carefully applied.

It was not until 11.18 hours that the Shannon supervisor issued instructions for an attempt to contact EI-AOM by radio. Cork ATC made three transmissions between 11.20 and 11.21 hours, including one on the emergency frequency of 121.5 MHz, and all with no response. A further delay ensued until 11.36 hours, when the off-duty senior ATC officer was informed of the situation at his home. He did not arrive at Shannon until about 12.15 hours, more than one and a quarter hours after the distress call.

It should be stated that an inaccurate transcript could have no possible effect on the flight, nor could it contribute in any way to the accident. If the typed radio records are flawed, for whatever reason, the major effect was to create a barrier which obstructed the 1970 team of investigators. It follows, *per se*, that they were also the breeding ground for the persistent rumours about the presence near Fethard of another aircraft or guided missile. In reality those sightings were of the disabled Viscount, and it is now quite clear to see how the mistaken belief in a second airborne object gained currency.

The French team did not allow themselves the degree of conjecture employed by me in the foregoing paragraphs. Yet it is only to be expected that individuals will construct their own theories in an attempt to reconcile the conflict between the new track and the radio signals. It is vaguely possible that during the bedlam which ensued after the crash, a staff member at Shannon could have accidentally selected the wrong tape for use in the preparation of the transcript. This could lead to use of a tape which was relevant to an earlier Cork to London flight, perhaps days or weeks before. There is a subtle pointer to indicate that this is a possible, if unlikely, explanation. While reporting points, altitude data and times may share some common language with other flights on that service from Cork to London, there is one critical variable component. It is the time of takeoff.

If a previous tape was inadvertently selected, then it must have referred to an aircraft which took off five minutes earlier than the fatal flight. There was a limit to the time available for preparation of the transcript. The date of certification on the document is 25 March 1968, the day after the crash. In this atmosphere of haste, those who prepared the transcript could have missed the fact that an estimated time of 11.03 hours for arrival at Strumble does not match the takeoff time of 10.32 hours in the undoubted Cork Control Tower transcript for the morning of 24 March 1968. If the wrong tape was accidentally picked out, then it must have referred to an aircraft which had enjoyed expeditious passenger and baggage loading, and unhindered taxi track to the take-off holding point. As that flight rotated off the Cork runway at the earlier time of 10.27 hours, the first thread would be woven in the erroneous pathways and con-clusions which would follow.

It is a great irony that, while the 2002 study finally eliminated the rumours of collision with an errant guided missile or target drone, a replacement mystery was perforce expounded which may yet be the subject of similar arguments in the years ahead.

27

Facing the
Appalling Vista

In the case of EI-AOM, it was beginning to look as though the entire truth had not been available to the 1970 inquiry team. Indirectly, the errors in the Shannon transcript had created the illusory flight of a second airborne object above south-east Ireland. Our maligned island neighbours not only seemed innocent of any stray missile launch and cover-up, but the Royal Navy had obviously made supreme efforts during the salvage operations, in conditions which had been made very difficult for them by Irish officials. The latter had created salvage time limitations and stingy budget restrictions. Any objective study of the contemporaneous UK files will exonerate the erstwhile alleged villains.

The conclusions by Exp'Air which concern the Shannon Area ATC radio transcripts are indeed an appalling vista to consider, but they must be seriously viewed as a real possibility because of the very persuasive case advanced by the international team of experts. The reconstructed track of EI-AOM, carefully based on statements by the forty-six witnesses, including some who answered a call to come forward in 2000, is now universally accepted as accurate. There remains, however, a small camp of doubters who claim that the Viscount was under perfect control as it meandered low above the counties of Waterford and Wexford. There is a school of thought which asserts that the captain deliberately departed from the flight plan, choosing instead to divert on a low-level, sightseeing tour, perhaps at the behest of an American passenger who was anxious to view the old Kennedy homestead in County Wexford. The hypothesis put forward by these dissenters includes an allegation that the crew transmitted two false radio messages to Shannon that they were level at 17,000 feet. As a writer I thought long and hard about some suitable method to deal with this dissent. It would be unfaithful to the book if I totally ignored it. Equally, it would be hypocritical if I wrote in favour of that theory, as I consider the findings of the 2002 study to be more credible. In the end I felt that the most appropriate course is to present both arguments, and allow the reader to examine the evidence within the confines of an imaginary jury room.

Exp'Air were aware of the rumours of a controlled departure from the flight plan and they did not shirk a very detailed study of the issue. The arguments which comprise Appendix 3 of this volume are verbatim extracts from the 2002 study. Part A comprises an analysis to determine if the flight patterns and maneouvres observed by the witnesses were those of an intact Viscount under unimpaired pilot control, and which had deviated deliberately from the flight plan. Part B examines the proposition that EI-AOM had suffered an initial upset at about 10.42 hours above Old Parish, and that for the remainder of the flight it was flown in a disabled condition. Part C is an attempt to establish whether or not the radio transcripts reflect a true picture of the flight path of the Viscount.

28

The Lucky Country

———————

Colin Torkington was an important member of the international team which delivered its conclusions in the 2002 study. Since the other team members were French, it can be questioned how an Australian with strong English connections became involved. When dealing with an air accident which dates back three decades, it is helpful to have access to a man who lived through that era and who worked in the industry. A modern whiz kid weaned on computer cockpits and wide-body jets is about as useful as an ashtray on a motorcycle when he is faced with the Vickers Viscount.

Colin was born in Yorkshire and began his career with Vickers-Armstrong, progressing to the post of senior stressman in the design office of that company. After moving to Australia in 1961, he was involved as structures group leader during the investigation of two Viscount crashes caused by structural failure. (An outline of his life and qualifications is set out under 'Investigation Team, 2000' on pages xxxii–xxxiii.)

The Viscount was constructed by using a philosophy wherein any primary structural elements which were at risk from fatigue failure had a 'safe life' allocated to them, and they were replaced at specific intervals.

Modern airliners are built with a belt-and-braces approach called 'fail-safe'. If any individual element fails from crack propagation or other cause, adjacent components take up the load and avoid catastrophic failure of the rest of the airframe.

God alone knows how many lives the Australian aviation safety authorities saved with the stroke of a pen in 1969. Shortly after the loss of EI-AOM, they shocked the world of aviation by banning all Viscount 700 Series aircraft from their skies, and by introducing stringent requirements for any future flights of the 800 Series. It was a unilateral move without precedent in air commerce. Emphatically they ordered operators of the 700 Series to remove their fleets entirely from the air register, and they issued demanding directives to any airline willing to continue flying the newer Viscounts. Old nostalgic Commonwealth links with Mother England were ignored in the rejection of the British airliner. As far as the Australians were concerned, this was a suspect aeroplane.

The first Australian Viscount 720, newly delivered from the Vickers production line, crashed during a crew training exercise at Mangalore. Three of the eight men on board died in that Trans Australia Airlines aircraft on 31 October 1954. Another 720, this time from the Ansett-ANA fleet, crashed into Botany Bay when the starboard outer wing folded upwards. In that accident, on 30 November 1961, all fifteen persons on board died. By now the 800 series had arrived, and on 22 September 1966 an Ansett-ANA 832 suffered an unusual fire caused by a loose oil-metering unit. The flames spread to a fuel tank, weakening the wing spar. None of the twenty-four souls on board survived the subsequent crash. Within a short period a third Viscount 720 of MacRobertson Miller Airlines crashed on 31 December 1968. Once again a wing spar had failed, and this time there were twenty-six deaths.

Airworthiness directives were now coming thick and fast, prompted by additional worldwide problems experienced in the tail and other parts. These were the same ADs which found their way to Aer Lingus and to all airlines operating Viscount fleets. While their American, European and other counterparts were content to try to deal with each AD as it arrived, the Australian air safety authorities were aghast at the formidable number of warnings. They decided that the maintenance tasks and modifications required for continued operation of the Viscounts were becoming too demanding. They chose instead to ground the ailing aircraft fleets. No other person would be allowed to die in a Viscount within Australia.

The Australians have always striven courageously to maintain a very high standard of air safety. Though the decision was controversial at the time, they did not hesitate when it came to urgent action about the Viscount fleets. Temporary certificates of airworthiness were issued to enable the empty banned aircraft to be flown out of the country. After 1969, a further sixty-eight Viscounts were destined to be lost in other countries, with dreadful carnage. But Australian hands were clean. All they could do was to look after their own patch of blue, and their own citizens.

29

A Captain at Work

The commander of Flight 712 stalks every facet of the 2002 study in a manner not unlike the ghost of Hamlet's father on the ramparts of Elsinore. His presence begins with the poignant sound bite of six words, spoken at 10.58 hours and preserved for ever on the iron oxide coating of an old tape from a recording apparatus in London. That message has been copied on to space-age laser discs, to be studiously examined by acoustic analysts. The syllables have undulated as waves on the green screens of oscilloscopes. It is listened to at various speeds, over and over again. In the end it told us very little about the final spin, and nothing at all about the captain.

I made a conscious decision quite early in my research activities for Exp'Air to gain some detailed appreciation of the life of the captain. Indeed his personality type was to become a matter of intense debate within the pages of the 2002 study, when it became necessary to form a conclusion on whether or not he was capable of transmitting two spurious radio signals.

While some men and women choose to become farmers, chefs, poets or hairdressers, there are others who take on the onerous task of flight training, with all the sacrifices and dedicated purpose which the work of an airline pilot demands. The world of commercial aviation is a small and incestuous place. Pilots, in particular, can become the targets of rumours, usually baseless. There were persistent suggestions that the crew of EI-AOM had ignored the flight plan to undertake a sightseeing tour. Even the partners and spouses of long-haul pilots are sometimes exposed to gossip concerning an imagined peccadillo by their loved one in a far-flung crew hotel. The real truth is usually that of an aviator exhausted by the demands of tight schedules, technical snags, crowded skies, dehydration, and an internal clock out of kilter with the local populace. A working day spent at the tip of the arrow, with 300 trusting souls strapped to his or her back, leaves little yearning for the high life after touchdown. Top of the desired list is a hot shower, a meal which is not pre-cooked and reheated in a galley, and somewhere comfortable to get your head down.

In the first few lines of Section 5.4.3.3 of the study report, Exp'Air refer to Captain O'Beirne as an 'ex-combat' pilot. From this they infer that the derring-do exploits associated with that role can result in a casual attitude to safety. This devil's advocacy proposition was made by them in their examination of the theory of false position reporting during the fatal flight. The captain, however, never flew in combat. Exp'Air probably intended to write 'ex-military', and a misnomer arose within their use of English, a language foreign to them. It is a good example of the way a canard can gain currency. The captain did train in the IAC. I have not sighted his military records, but I examined his civil logbooks, kindly loaned to me by his son. In the section which refers to 'Previous Experience' he mentions his past military hours aloft. His *ab initio* training was on the Chipmunk, a docile tandem-seat tutor with the same engine as a Tiger Moth biplane. He also flew the T.51

Provost, a more advanced piston trainer. His multi-engine experience was limited to a 1935 design, the Avro Anson XII, an unwieldy utility aircraft often used for navigation training.

The only high-performance aircraft flown by Captain O'Beirne was the Spitfire IX. It is likely that his limited hours in that legendary fighter would have included deliberate inducement of spins, followed by difficult recoveries. This exposure, together with spin exercises on the Chipmunk and Provost, would have conditioned his reflexes to an instant recognition of auto-rotation, and may well have helped in his unique recovery of EI-AOM from its spins or spiral dives. Spin recovery in a Spitfire is no cakewalk.

Anecdotal references from the 1950s era at Baldonnel military training airfield, however, indicate that it may be unwise to attribute too much significance to the captain's hours logged on Spitfires. At that time, work was not completed on the concrete runway, and for much of the year the soggy ground was unsuitable for a fighter with a narrow wheel track and lacking in wide low-pressure tyres. The engine was a Rolls-Royce Merlin 66, a thirsty twelve-cylinder beast of immense power. It is likely that budget restrictions ensured that only essential hours were logged, and there were few, if any, opportunities for joy flights made with aerobatic abandon. His total number of hours in all IAC machines was a modest 235.

On his departure from the IAC he began immediate duties with Aer Lingus at the age of twenty-three. On 16 April 1956 he started a conversion course on the Douglas DC-3, which he completed in fifteen hours, including one hour at night. Thereafter, he flew as 'Pilot under Supervision' with Captains Barrett, Mackay, Cregg, White, Kelly, Bourke, Harkin, Foot, Conway, Green, Martin, Jackson, Quin, MacAlinden, Brown, Allen, McKeown, and many other wiser and older flyers who would have instilled in him the attributes required of an airline pilot — nice and gentle with the power, smooth climb and descent, no split-arse turns, and grease it on to the runway. He dutifully served his apprenticeship in the right-hand seat of that superb piston engine workhorse. The DC-3 is not a pressurised aircraft which flies high above the weather. By day and night he honed his skills in the abysmal meteorological conditions which so often pervade the lower altitudes of these islands, a routine broken only by an occasional charter foray to Lourdes.

It was on 1 July 1958 that he first flew a Viscount, designated EI-AJI. His logged time had by now reached 1,000 hours. In some weeks he alternated daily within the cockpits of Viscounts, Fokker Friendships and DC-3s. It is a measure of the man that despite his access to sophisticated turboprop aircraft, his log-books reveal that on his days off he would steal away to spend time flying a tiny old Chipmunk. By sporadically renewing the relationship with his first paramour, he is revealed as a man who truly loved flying. It is extraordinary how many airline pilots emulate that same trait. In Sydney I would occasionally get a phone call from one Rudi Camillo on a day when he was not flying a DC-9 jet. We would drive out to Bankstown airfield and share the cost of renting a small Piper Cherokee for an hour. We flew like excited kids along the Pacific beaches between Botany Bay and Broken Bay, with occasional glimpses of sharks in the waters below us.

On 28 January 1961 Bernard O'Beirne crewed his first transatlantic jet flight in a Boeing 720, a variant of the ground-breaking popular 707 type. Thus began a period when he added to his navigation skills and instrument flying on trips to Boston, New York and Montreal. On 22 December 1961 his Boeing 720 aircraft EI-ALA established a record time of 5 hours 43 minutes for the ocean crossing, landing in New York. As 1964 drew to a close, he was chosen for promotion to command duty, and he began a series of flights to be checked out for suitability and skill. At 5.25 on the dark winter evening of 25 January 1965, his years as a co-pilot ended as he opened the twin throttles of Fokker Friendship EI-AKA to lift off for Edinburgh. He returned to Dublin at 10.50 pm and so began his short remaining years in command of Viscounts and Fokkers. His total flying hours had now reached 5,000.

EI-AOM was one of a number of Viscounts purchased by Aer Lingus from KLM in November 1966. It had served in the fleet of that Dutch airline for ten years, and had 16,586 flying hours accumulated on the airframe. On 28 February 1967 Captain O'Beirne first flew the aircraft in which he would die one year later. Its sister ship EI-AOF crashed during a training flight above County Meath on 22 June 1967, killing three of O'Beirne's colleagues.

There may be some who will say that I wrote this chapter in an attempt to protect the memory and good name of Bernard O'Beirne, and they may well be right. I became quite depressed for a short time in September 2002 when a revised version of the original rumour of a flight plan deviation began to circulate in Dublin. The fresh assertion of an unauthorised change in the plan has been adjusted to reconcile with the track of EI-AOM as reconstructed in the 2002 study. It would not be of great concern if the diversion theory was being peddled by barrack-room lawyers in pubs, or by those who would not know the pointy end of an aircraft from the tail. It came as a shock to me when a senior person within the cogs of a government department, a man whom I admire and respect, put it to me that it was true. He is not alone.

The bottom line is the fact that those who espouse the validity of the diversion story are asking us to accept a hypothesis which besmirches the names of Captain O'Beirne and his young co-pilot, Paul Heffernan. It includes a spin-off of pain for their families. One of the many small things which stood out clearly as I studied the dead captain's log-books was the punctilious manner in which every detail of his flying career is set out; each hour was carefully recorded as his proficiency grew. In the column allowed for remarks he details the names of the wise old check captains who monitored his progress on the flight deck, reporting their observations to the chief pilot, the man who nominated the impressive co-pilot as suitable material for the responsibilities of a command in the left-hand seat. This is not an automatic promotion, simply based on years of service or on hard-won totals of hours. The personality type is critical in the earning of four gold stripes.

By March of 1968 O'Beirne had become a father for the second time and his young son was not yet two years old. As a career pilot he viewed his responsibilities to his family, and to his duties within a cramped workplace, with equal profundity. For relaxation he played golf, and it came as no surprise to me that he applied the same dedication to that art as to his flying. By the time he died he was playing off scratch.

Yet the rumour mill has proposed that on Sunday 24 March 1968 this man suddenly changed his personality. It is claimed that he engaged in a series of flight manoeuvres which would be anathema to his dedicated professionalism, and that he and his aspiring young apprentice both lied by radio to cover up these defalcations. It is said that during the ascent through 9,000 feet above Old Parish he suddenly decided to abort the climb, rolled his four-engine turboprop sharply to the right with fifty-seven passengers aboard, and plunged almost vertically in a spin or spiral dive to low altitude. Following other flight patterns which at times took the

Viscount below cliff level, and which stressed the airframe beyond its design limitations, it is suggested that he flew inland to be seen by churchgoers to barely avoid collision with the church steeple. He deliberately descended under perfect control, so the doubters say, to a level so low that the grass was flattened by the wash from the propeller thrust. I simply cannot buy it.

There is a flying book much loved by aviators, written by Ernest K. Gann and titled *Fate is the Hunter*. Chapter 17 begins with a telling message which should cause us all to reflect deeply. It reads:

> The urge to shift blame becomes even uglier when the accused has left the feast.

30

Shooting the Messenger

T he ink was scarcely dry on the first draft of the 2002 study when the objections began. Exp'Air were rocking the boat and it soon became obvious that it had suited some vested interests to have the old missile fairy tale to rely on. Draft copies were circulated to all interested parties, and soon the first of the written responses began to surface. In some cases there was repudiation of isolated sections of the study. Others rejected the conclusions in their entirety. The corporate successors to Vickers, BAE Systems, put up a good case in defence of the design integrity, which ran to seventeen pages. Yet its letter to Exp'Air on 16 August 2001 lost its effect in some paragraphs by including pedantic jibes at occasional grammatical or spelling errors observed in the draft. Overall, the French had provided an easily understood English text. It was, after all, a technical study and did not aspire to join the short list for the Booker Prize.

The IAA was not happy either. It quickly asserted that the accident pre-dated the formation of IAA, and it entered pleas in its letter of 14 January 2002, addressed to the Department of Public Enterprise. The tenor was akin to the waiter in a popular television series — 'I know nothing. I am from Barcelona.' It emulated the BAE criticism of the text translation, ignoring the fact that it was perfectly good enough to make them understand that Exp'Air was making a recommendation for a change in practice which affected the present structures. IAA sprang to the defence of the two Shannon ATC staff, mentioned anonymously in the French analysis of the radio tape transcripts. It declared the extensive 2002 study to be nothing more than a 'retrospective informal investigation, conducted without any new evidence'. But this was patently untrue. New witnesses had answered a call to come forward, and their testimony had been married by Exp'Air to some accounts by the 1968 observers, whose affidavits had been rejected by the 1970 inquiry board. While experience shows that some persons present in the vicinity of any accident, be it of a ship, car, or aircraft, can make occasional errors in their recollection of events at the time, it is clear that this was a different situation. The new track is not based on the word of a paltry few. Forty-six individuals affirmed sights and sounds which provided a clear and logical sequence. As a large group they made up a very reliable and corroborative jury. The fresh witnesses were not relying on a recollection of events from three decades ago. They had been repeating the very same claims relentlessly down the years, and some were still angry at the continued rejection of their potential contributions which they had always felt certain were significant. It was a relief to them to have their testimony finally heard by Exp'Air, and inserted decisively into the appropriate sector of the new track reconstruction.

Everybody with an axe to grind was now questioning the French presentation of the flight track, but nobody was coming up with an alternative explanation for the plethora of sightings between Old Parish, Tory Hill and Fethard. There was also new data from the post-1970 experience of the maintenance management of Viscount fleets, and from comparative accidents in those intervening years, including the 1980 Indonesian disaster of considerable relevance. The IAA letter added an unconvincing suggestion that the type of study conducted by Exp'Air might damage 'the well-tested statutory aircraft accident procedures of the State'. Even persons who have only tenuous connections with the world of aviation are fully aware of the differences between an official ICAO Annex 13 inquiry and the less formal types of review or study. It is difficult to imagine how any damage could be caused. The IAA ignored the fact that it was the informal review of files conducted by the AAIU in 1999 that had made some astounding and incontrovertible discoveries relating to the maintenance procedures within Aer Lingus. It also conveniently avoided the glaring fact that it was just such a 'statutory' inquiry which in 1970 had fostered the paranoid Brit-bashing theory of collision with an errant target drone or missile, now conclusively shown to be arrant nonsense within the 1999 review and the 2002 study. The 1970 statutory inquiry had also failed to question, or had not spotted, the many anomalies in the Shannon radio transcript.

Also ignored by the IAA was the culture which allowed the original 1968 investigation team to be headed by the same man who, shortly before the crash, had approved the Certificate of Airworthiness for EI-AOM. That important document was based on defective paperwork and on maintenance records known to be missing at the time of its issue. Yet when the astonishing overruns in the mandatory compliance periods between inspections of various components of EI-AOM were revealed in a secret review of such procedures, immediately after the disaster, no mention of these potentially disastrous errors was made in the official 1970 report. In fact, the suspicion raised by that incomprehensible omission from a vaunted inquiry, clothed in 'statutory' guise, was one of the reasons why the 2002 study had been delegated to a foreign triumvirate by the Minister for Public Enterprise, Mary O'Rourke. This step was taken to ensure independence of its functions, and the removal of cronyism, nepotism or other such undue influences. It is no wonder that the IAA is seeking to distance itself from its predecessors.

Two days before the release date of the study a letter arrived by fax at the AAIU from Vincent Toher and Company, acting under instructions from the Shannon air traffic controller who had been on duty between 08.30 and 10.55 GMT on the morning of the crash. The letter was brief and entered a simple rejection by their client of the contents of the draft report in those areas which related to him. It reiterated the veracity of his statement to Exp'Air and relied on the fact that the tape transcripts had been duly certified as correct. There was no attempt to provide any explanation for the various discrepancies relating to text, timings, continuity and behaviour patterns which have been identified in the Shannon transcript. In fairness to the controller, it is likely that he was acting under legal advice to phrase his denial in the simplest possible terms. Lawyers have a tendency to operate on the principle of minimal disclosure.

It is a depressing exercise to look at the manner in which some state institutions and other parties seek to protect themselves when confronted with credible conclusions such as those which form part of the 2002 study. They engage in a type of 'evasion-speak', which is aimed solely at guarding their butts. It all becomes tedious and predictable, bearing close resemblance to the round-table conferences in *Yes, Minister*. The enormous volume of work carried out by Exp'Air with honesty, integrity and skill is not acknowledged by such cliques.

Instead they seek any available avenue of criticism and take a child-like delight in launching petty barbs to confuse the issues. They lack the courage to present any alternative hypothesis, and provided they can escape unscathed from any potential culpability, they close ranks behind a screen of 'I'm all right, Jack.' Thus it would be naive to expect that such persons would have the fortitude to raise their heads above the parapet and offer some explanations to the relatives of the sixty-one who died. Why, for instance, are there no expressions of regret about the past mistakes? Somebody should surely acknowledge that it was totally inappropriate to have the 1970 investigation team headed by the man who had approved the Certificate of Airworthiness in dubious circumstances. They could at least apologise for the fact that any mention of the known errors in the Maintenance Plan was mysteriously omitted from the final report in 1970. It is evasive on their part to try to justify these transgressions by saying that some other airlines made similar errors in that era, as has been asserted. The loved ones of the surviving relatives did not die in an aircraft of those other fleets.

There is a thought which nags at me, and does not easily go away. There exists a remote possibility that the original setting up of a new study was viewed as a placebo exercise to quiet the persistent voices and demands of the families of the victims. After all, it was a 1968 accident in Ireland and there was no real prospect of a French-led team shedding any further light on the enigma after a lapse of thirty-two years.

In the final paragraph of his letter of 14 January 2002 to the Department of Public Enterprise, the chief executive of the IAA makes bleating noises about the anomalies in the Shannon radio transcript, pinpointed by Exp'Air in the study conclusions. He is concerned that the revelation of the inconsistencies, and the inferences which naturally follow, could damage the reputations of unnamed but potentially identifiable former staff of Air Traffic Control. By itself, that may be a laudable anxiety. But what of those within government departments and allied institutions who continue to spread the gospel of an illegal departure from the flight plan by the pilots, and subsequent low-level controlled flight? Is there no concern about the effect these allegations have on the O'Beirne and Heffernan families? Or do the powers that be identify more readily with those of their own desk-bound ilk, considering the reputations of those with artisan flying skills to be of lesser value? Perhaps there are resentments because Exp'Air saw fit to draw special attention to the extraordinary skills and exploits of the two dead pilots, who kept a mortally wounded machine airborne for half an hour. There was no such honourable mention in the study for the men in high places who were charged with the duty of overseeing the Maintenance Plan, and none was deserved.

31

Janice and Dale

Some thousands of miles from Tuskar Rock lies one of the highest peaks in the world, called Tupungato. It is a volcanic mountain in the Andes region of Argentina, and close to the Chilean border. Its name means 'Storm Zone', and the flanks of the massive prominence are sheathed in glaciers. In January 2000 a party of mountaineers stumbled on the wreckage of an airliner, which had been reported missing on a flight from London. This was an Avro 691 Lancastrian 3, a derivative of the legendary Lancaster bomber, and powered by four V-12 Rolls-Royce Merlin engines. It was registered G-AGWH, and named *Star Dust* by its operators, British South American Airways. The bodies of some passengers, preserved in the ice, were found in the main wreckage. This discovery on the eastern slopes made it possible to determine the final descent course towards Santiago Airport and to confirm the probable cause of the accident. The pattern of damage to the blades of a recovered propeller showed that its engine had been throttled back somewhat at impact. Undetected strong headwinds had led to a premature descent in darkness, after the crew thought they had already passed safely over the high peaks.

On the face of it, this does not appear to be a singularly noteworthy event. What makes it so significant is the fact that the aircraft had crashed on 2 August 1947, driving itself deep into the ice at 16,000 feet above sea level. During the fifty-three years that followed, the glacier had crept down the slope at snail's pace, until it reached a sharp rise in the valley floor. Thereupon the wreckage was inexorably forced to the surface of the ice cover, and slowly expelled into view.

The pessimists say that the cause of the initial damage to the left tailplane of Aer Lingus Viscount EI-AOM above Old Parish will never be resolved. Yet I believe that it will. On that Sunday morning in 1968, some tailplane section, which we need to enable resolution of the last remaining part of the puzzle, did not disappear for ever. It is simply missing, and lies somewhere on the sea bed or on land. One day, perhaps tomorrow, the sands which have probably silted over it will be scoured away again by the freak current of a storm tide, and an unsuspecting trawler crew will snag the priceless artefact. The spars of the Viscount tailplane were robust alloy load-carriers, and do not disappear like the more vulnerable magnesium components of an aircraft, which erode rapidly in salt water. With modern methods of analysis it is quite feasible that a section of spar or web plate will still reveal any tell-tale evidence of flutter damage, corrosion, fatigue crack propagation, or bird strike, even after many decades in the sea. If such detail is absent, the break-up pattern can usually be determined by the sheer physical sufferance of any recovered piece, after the protective coating of marine growth encrustation or earthen casing is removed.

The Andean discovery is not unique in the annals of aviation history, and similar sites of debris have been found many decades after crashes in Australia, the Sahara and other remote places. There is ample evidence that many items of wreckage from EI-AOM, collected by souvenir hunters from the beach at Greenore Point shortly after the disaster, may still lie hidden in private homes, outhouses and garden sheds. This is a personal conviction, triggered by my own retrieval of more than a dozen such pieces during the very limited search foray I made into rural Wexford during October 2000. In one case, where tenure had changed hands, the new occupier was not even aware of the genesis of a strange item left in the attic by a forgetful former tenant. Even as I write, I am aware that some farmer who reads these words may suddenly recall a strange metallic object which he discovered on his land some years ago. It now lies within a heap of scrap metal pieces — short lengths of tubular scaffolding, gate sections and steel bars, and other such bits and pieces which are saved and accumulate on thrifty farms.

It is probable that all or sections of the left elevator and tabs, followed by the left tailplane, fell into the sea or penetrated the ground on farmland. Such an item may be ploughed up again or trawled in a serendipitous discovery to provide the final answer. We must not forget that it took all of thirty-four years just to establish that EI-AOM had suffered her initial upset above County Waterford, and not within a stone's throw of the Welsh coast.

There was one such miraculous discovery by a farmer. In 1989 a crippled DC-10 jet airliner diverted to a heavy crash landing on a runway at Sioux City Airport, after the tail-mounted engine had exploded and destroyed the adjacent hydraulic lines, which led to loss of all the primary flight controls. With incredible skill, the pilots managed limited control for half an hour by using only variations of power on the two remaining wing-mounted engines. Despite many deaths, they saved the lives of 184 people on board. When the wreckage was examined it was discovered that a critical fan disc was missing from within the exploded engine, and if it could be found it would help to solve the crash cause. It had fallen to earth from 37,000 feet, somewhere above the maize belt of Iowa. In that hinterland the corn grows 'as high as an elephant's eye', just as in *Oklahoma*. A reward was offered for its recovery, but little hope was held out by the FAA, as the odds were astronomical in those vast expanses.

Three months after the crash an Iowa farmer named Dale Sorensen, together with his wife Janice, were working a John Deere combine harvester which takes six rows of corn at a time. They hit something solid. Janice backed up and dismounted to investigate an arc of metal protruding just above the ground. She had heard about the reward and she correctly guessed that it was indeed the fan disc. The heavy assembly was buried deep in the soil after falling from a height of seven miles. Later microscopic analysis revealed the tiny casting flaw, no bigger than a pinprick, which had initiated the fracture and crack propagation in the titanium structure.

I harbour a very special reason for believing that a part of the tailplane from EI-AOM will surface somewhere at a future date. Compare the immense areas of Iowa, traversed by the DC-10 at 37,000 feet, with the small acreage of the reconstructed flight path of the Viscount at low altitude, above the compact rural stretches of southern Ireland and the adjacent sea. The mathematical odds of finding the fan disc in those vast sweeping cornfields of America, and among endless tall swathes of maize plants, were colossal. In the relatively tiny farmland region of south-east Ireland, and the narrow adjoining triangle of water between Carnsore Point, Tuskar Rock lighthouse, and the Saltee Islands, we have placed a long-term wager at much better odds than in Iowa. A shout may yet echo from a trawler deck, or from a farmer transfixed by a glinting piece of metal, jettisoned by a ploughshare.

Appendix 1

THE RADIO TRANSCRIPTS

Transcriptions of signals between EI-AOM and various ground stations (all times are GMT)

Cork Control Tower	10.26 hours to 10.33
Cork Approach	10.34 hours to 10.39
Shannon Control Area	10.39 hours to 10.57
London Airways	10.57 hours to 11.08
Cork Approach	11.20 hours to 11.21
Telephone line between Shannon and London	10.36 hours to 10.44

SYNOPSIS DERIVED FROM TEXT

Takeoff from Cork Airport was at 10.32 hours. The aircraft reached the assigned cruise altitude of 17,000 feet at 10.51 plus 48 seconds. At 10.57 plus 29 seconds the Viscount reached the start of the London Airways control zone, and a switch was made to the new radio frequency of 131.2 MHz. A signal was transmitted on the London frequency at 10.58 plus 2 seconds, when the aircraft was close to the Welsh coast. The call was couched in a most unusual format. It cited the phonetic registration letters of EI-AOM, rather than the normal flight number. A possible explanation for this may be that a sudden and highly stressful situation had already developed in the cockpit. This could cause the pilot to momentarily forget his flight number, which varies with each journey. The registration letters are permanently displayed in large clear characters on his instrument panel. Although not phrased as a standard distress call, it does indicate that something was already awry.

Eight seconds later, at 10.58 plus 10 seconds, all doubt was removed when the pilot reported that the aircraft was spinning and descending through 5,000 feet.

A loss of 12,000 feet in 8 seconds is not possible, a further indication that when the first call was made, the flight was already in peril. Later acoustic analysis of the weak transmission leaned more towards '12,000' being the altitude spoken within the signal, but even a loss of 5,000 feet in 8 seconds is not possible. (Findings within the 2002 study swung the pendulum back towards the original '5,000' signal.) The final distress call was intercepted by another Aer Lingus aircraft and by a BOAC flight, both of which immediately relayed it to London Airways.

The regulations required that the Shannon transcripts should have included all radio transmissions and telephone calls made up to the time when a Full Alert was declared. This occurred at 11.25 hours. Both of the Shannon transcripts stop prematurely. The reason for this is not known. The missing time period precludes examination of the subject matter of any further telephone conversations between Shannon and London after 10.44 hours. It is also impossible to ascertain if there were any readable or unreadable radio signals from EI-AOM to Shannon after 10.57 hours. The recordings were either lost or taped over again.

TRANSCRIPTION FROM THE TAPE RECORDING OF RADIO SIGNALS BETWEEN EI-AOM/CORK CONTROL TOWER AND EI-AOM/CORK APPROACH

Period: 10.26 GMT to 10.39 GMT, Sunday 24 March 1968

Note: 712 = call sign (flight number) of EI-AOM; TWR = Cork Airport Control Tower; 03 = 3 minutes past the next hour (e.g. 11.03 when spoken *after* 10.03). See also 'Abbreviations and Glossary' on page xvii.

Time	From	To	Recorded Intelligence
1026	EI712	TWR	712 Start
1026	TWR	712	712, cleared to start. QNH 998, Temp. plus 08
1030	EI712	TWR	Taxi clearance?
1030	EI712	TWR	Taxi?
1031	TWR	712	712 cleared to taxi, RW17
1031	TWR	712	ATC
1031	EI712	TWR	Go ahead
1031	TWR	712	Aer Lingus 712 is cleared Cork to London Airport, Airways Blue 10, Green 1, Flight Level 170.
1031	EI712	TWR	Blue 10, Green 1, 170.
1031	TWR	712	Your climb out will be left turn out, climbing on radial 102 until through Flight Level 100 on course.
1031	EI712	TWR	Roger, left turn out, radial 102 until 100, then on course
1031	TWR	712	Your traffic is a Herald inbound on radial 087, estimating Youghal 46, descending to 50.
1031	EI712	TWR	Roger
1032	TWR	712	Cleared takeoff. Left turn out, climb radial 102. Wind 200/13 knots.
1032	EI712	TWR	Left turn out on to radial 102
1033	TWR	712	712 was airborne at 32. Contact Approach 119.3
1033	EI712	TWR	Roger
1034	EI712	TWR	Cork Approach, 712
1034	APP	712	Climb as instructed. Call passing Flight Level 70, please.
1034	EI712	APP	Roger, will call passing 70
1035	GWC	APP	Cork, Whiskey Charlie is passing 70
1035	APP	GWC	OK, Whiskey Charlie. Advise again out of 60
1035	GWC	APP	Roger, will do
1036	APP	712	712, present level?

Time	From	To	Recorded Intelligence
1036	EI712	APP	60, climbing to 170
1037	APP	712	When out of 70, 712 is cleared turn left on course for Tuskar
1037	EI712	APP	Roger D
1038	EI712	APP	712 out of 70
1038	APP	712	Roger, 712. Cleared on course. Now change to Shannon 127.5. Over.
1039	EI712	APP	Cheerio.

TRANSCRIPTION OF SHANNON/EI-AOM RADIO TRANSMISSIONS ON 24 MARCH 1968

This is a certified transcript of recording of radio transmissions on Shannon Area Control frequency 127.5 MHz during the period 10.39 to 10.57 GMT, Sunday 24 March 1968. The transcript was dated at Shannon Airport on 25 March 1968.

Time	From	To	Text
1039:45	EI 712	Shannon	Shannon, 712, good morning.
	Shannon	EI 712	712, good morning.
	712	Shannon	By Youghal, passing through 75, climbing to 170, Tuskar 57.
1040:00	Shannon	712	Roger, 712, if you wish you may route direct to Strumble, go ahead.
	712	Shannon	(Unreadable)
	Shannon	712	Your transmission [sic] are fairly unreadable here. Confirm you are accepting a direct routing to Strumble.
	712	Shannon	Affirmative. Estimating Strumble at 03.
	Shannon	712	Roger, call cruising.
1041:20	Shannon	712	Your present level?

Time	From	To	Text
	712	Shannon	712 is passing 90.
	Shannon	712	Roger, arrange your climb to cross the boundary at 170.
	712	Shannon	(Unreadable)
1042:12	GAPMC	Shannon	Request permission return to Shannon. Flight level 100, over.
	Shannon	GAPMC	Cleared return Shannon. Maintain 100, report Foynes.
1043:15	EI 112	Shannon	And the 112 cruising 150
	Shannon	112	112, cleared Dublin 128.0
	112	Shannon	Cheerio
	Shannon	GAPMC	Cleared to leave 100 for flight level 55. Check out of 100.
	Shannon	GAPMC	Cleared to leave 100 for flight level 55. Call reaching 55.
1044:00	GAPMC	Shannon	Roger, cleared 55, leaving 100
1045:00	GAPMC	Shannon	Foynes, 80, descending, over
	Shannon	GAPMC	Roger, cleared VOR. Descend to 4,000. QNH 997. After VOR proceed out on localizer.
	GAPMC	Shannon	Roger, descending to 4,000. 997. Will call VOR station.
	Shannon	GAPMC	Cleared number 1, ILS approach, runway 24, expect no delay
	GAPMC	Shannon	Roger
1047:00	GAPMC	Shannon	4,000 feet
	Shannon	GAPMC	Change to 118.7. Tower will advise you of sequence.
1051:48	712	Shannon	Level at 170
	Shannon	712	Roger, report at Bannow

Time	From	To	Text
1057:07	712	Shannon	712 by Bannow. Level 170, estimating Strumble at 03.
	Shannon	712	Roger, say again the time by Bannow. I got the Strumble estimate OK
	712	Shannon	57
	Shannon	712	OK, time 56 and a half. Change now to London Airways 131.2. Good-day.
1057:29	712	Shannon	131.2. Good-

[Author's Note: For reasons unknown this transcript did not continue up to the regulatory time of 11.25 hours when the Full Alert was called.]

TRANSCRIPTION FROM THE TAPE RECORDING OF RADIO COMMUNICATIONS BETWEEN EI-AOM AND LONDON AIRWAYS

Period: 10.57 GMT to 11.07 GMT, on Sunday 24 March 1968

Notes: The text in this transcript is verbatim, and includes the spaces in the original. A brief period of total silence results in a blank line. The question marks denote indecipherable or garbled transmissions. The original upper case style has been preserved.

LIN 362 was another Aer Lingus aircraft, en route from Dublin to Bristol, when the upset of EI-AOM occurred. The crew overheard the distress call, and brought that fact to the attention of London Airways. Propagation of VHF radio signals is much clearer at altitude, particularly when there is line of sight between aircraft antennae.

LIN 362 later descended to 500 feet to search the sea surface, but saw nothing. The first hint of distress came at 10.58:02, in an unusual format using all five phonetic registration letters of the aircraft instead of the call sign '712'. 'Intercom' near a line of speech indicates an internal discussion between staff at London Airways control.

TO	FROM	RECORDED INTELLIGENCE	TIME (GMT)	REMARKS
LONDON AIRWAYS	LIN 362	LONDON AIRWAYS, AER LINGUS THREE SIX TWO		
LIN 362	LONDON AIRWAYS	THREE SIX TWO, AIRWAYS	10.57	
LONDON AIRWAYS	LIN 362	AER LINGUS THREE SIX TWO IS BY VARTRY AT FIVE SIX. LEVEL ONE THREE ZERO. STRUMBLE ZERO FIVE, FOR BRISTOL		
LIN 362	LONDON AIRWAYS	THREE SIX TWO, ROGER, ONE THREE ZERO, STRUMBLE GREEN ONE, BRISTOL		
LONDON AIRWAYS	LIN 362	ROGER		
LONDON RADAR	TC	TANGO CHARLIE NINE ZERO		
	??	— CHARLIE WILL YOU MOVE ??? ??? ???		
TC	LONDON RADAR	ROGER, TANGO CHARLIE		
	??	??? BREAKING UP OVER — ??? — ON STANDBY, CALLING YOU OVER — THAT'S BETTER. THANKS, ER, WILL YOU TRY TO CONTACT		Jammed, part — simultaneous.

TO	FROM	RECORDED INTELLIGENCE	TIME (GMT)	REMARKS
		THE TECH' IN CHARGE AT SIGNALS ??? ??? ??? ??? ???		
BOA 506	LONDON RADAR	SPEEDBIRD FIVE OH SIX IS FURTHER CLEARED TO SIX ZERO. WHAT'S YOUR PRESENT LEVEL?		
LONDON RADAR	BOA 506	OUT OF ONE FOUR ZERO, CLEARED TO SIX ZERO	1058	Simultaneous transmissions, — broke off.
	LIN 712	— ECHO INDIA ALPHA OSCAR MIKE WITH YOU —	1058:02	
BOA	LONDON RADAR	THANK YOU		
	??	— FINISHED		Origin unknown.
	LIN 712	— FIVE THOUSAND FEET, DESCENDING, SPINNING AT [sic] RAPIDLY	1058:10	Poor transmission.
LONDON RADAR	TC	LONDON, TANGO CHARLIE		
TC	LONDON RADAR	TANGO CHARLIE		
LONDON RADAR	TC	ER, FIVE EIGHT WOODLEY. CHERTSEY AT ZERO ONE		
		FINISHED		Intercom
		YEP		Intercom
TC	LONDON AIRWAYS	TANGO CHARLIE, LONDON. NOW ONE TWO SEVEN DECIMAL SEVEN		

TO	FROM	RECORDED INTELLIGENCE	TIME (GMT)	REMARKS
LONDON AIRWAYS	TC	ONE TWENTY-SEVEN SEVEN GOOD DAY		
TC	LONDON AIRWAYS	'DAY		
LONDON AIRWAYS	LIN 362	ER, LONDON FROM AER LINGUS THREE SIX TWO		
LIN 362	LONDON AIRWAYS	THREE SIXTY TWO, GO AHEAD		
LONDON AIRWAYS	LIN 362	ER, DID YOU JUST GET THAT MESSAGE ON THAT AIRCRAFT DESCENDING FROM FIVE THOUSAND FEET, SPINNING RAPIDLY. OVER?		
LIN 362	LONDON AIRWAYS	NO, WE DIDN'T COPY THAT. WOULD YOU SAY AGAIN THE MESSAGE		
LONDON AIRWAYS	LIN 362	WE JUST RECEIVED A BROKEN TRANSMISSION, ERRR, AIRCRAFT SPINNING RAPIDLY, GOING THROUGH FIVE THOUSAND FEET. ER, I DIDN'T GET THE CALL-SIGN. IT'S – GO AHEAD	1059	
LIN 362	LONDON AIRWAYS	ROGER, WE HEARD A TRANSMISSION BUT, ER, W-W-WE THOUGHT IT WAS A BREAKTHROUGH ON THE FREQUENCY		
LONDON AIRWAYS	LIN 362	IT MAY HAVE BEEN		

TO	FROM	RECORDED INTELLIGENCE	TIME (GMT)	REMARKS
LIN 362	LONDON AIRWAYS	AER LINGUS THREE SIX TWO, YOU DIDN'T HAPPEN TO COPY THE CALL-SIGN, DID YOU?		
LONDON AIRWAYS	LIN 362	WELL WE THOUGHT IT WAS, ER, OSCAR MIKE		
LIN 362	LONDON AIRWAYS	OK, THANK YOU		
LONDON AIRWAYS	BOA 506	ER, FIVE OH SIX IS OUT OF ONE ZERO THOUSAND FOR SEVEN ZERO AND, ER, STILL ON THE HEADING OF ONE SIXTY AS GIVEN. WE HEARD THE LAST PART OF HIS TRANSMISSION. HE WAS DESCENDING RAPIDLY. WE DIDN'T HEAR A CALL-SIGN.	1100	
BOA 506	LONDON	ER, FIVE OH SIX, ROGER, THANK YOU		
BOA 506	LONDON RADAR	FIVE OH SIX, NEXT CHECK PASSING SEVEN ZERO. CONTINUE YOUR HEADING FOR THE MOMENT.		
LONDON RADAR	BOA 506	FIVE OH SIX		
LONDON AIRWAYS	G-HE	ER, LONDON, GOLF HOTEL ECHO PASSED, ER, STANDBY ONE —		
		I'VE FINISHED WITH HIM		Intercom
		OK		Intercom

TO	FROM	RECORDED INTELLIGENCE	TIME (GMT)	REMARKS
LONDON AIRWAYS	G-HE	ER, LONDON, GOLF HOTEL ECHO PASSED WOODLEY AT ZERO ONE. ER, FLIGHT LEVEL ONE FIVE ZERO DUNSFOLD AT ZERO SEVEN		
G-HE	LONDON AIRWAYS	HOTEL ECHO, LONDON, ONE TWO SEVEN DECIMAL SEVEN		
LONDON AIRWAYS	G-HE	— TWO SEVEN SEVEN, ROGER		
			1101	Channel quiet
		RADAR YOU KNOW THAT BREAK —		(Intercom) Stopped as BOA 506 called.
LONDON RADAR	BOA 506	SPEEDBIRD FIVE OH SIX, LEVELLING AT SIX ZERO		
BOA 506	LONDON RADAR	ROGER, FIVE OH SIX		
		RADAR, ON THE BREAK-THROUGH, DID, ER, YOU KNOW THAT TRANSMISSION, DID YOU HEAR ANYTHING ON IT AT ALL?		Intercom
		NO, ONLY THE SPINNING BIT. I DIDN'T GET ANYTHING ELSE		Intercom
		YOU GOT THE SPINNING, DID YOU?		Intercom
		YEAH		Intercom
		YEH, OK, THANK YOU		Intercom

TO	FROM	RECORDED INTELLIGENCE	TIME (GMT)	REMARKS
LONDON RADAR	TWA 705	LONDON RADAR, TWA SEVEN OH FIVE WITH YOU		
TWA 705	LONDON RADAR	SEVEN OH FIVE, RADAR. FOUR THOUSAND FEET FOR THE MOMENT. ADVISE PASSING THREE	1102	
LONDON RADAR	TWA 705	ER, WILL DO		
		RADAR, WAS THE ONLY WORD YOU HEARD, SPINNING?		Intercom
		SPINNING AND RAPIDLY, ER, THAT WAS ALL		Intercom
		YES, OK		Intercom
BOA 506	LONDON RADAR	SPEEDBIRD FIVE OH SIX, RADAR. WILL YOU TURN LEFT FOR GARSTON NOW. THE QDM IS ZERO EIGHT ZERO		
LONDON RADAR	BOA 506	FIVE OH SIX, DIRECT GARSTON. THANK YOU		
LONDON AIRWAYS	LIN 362	ER, LONDON, AERLINGUS THREE SIX TWO. DO YOU HAVE AN AER LINGUS SEVEN ONE TWO OR SEVEN ONE THREE ON THE FREQUENCY?		
LIN 362	LONDON AIRWAYS	ER, THERE'S A SEVEN ONE TWO ON		
LONDON AIRWAYS	LIN 362	ER, ROGER		

Appendix 1

TO	FROM	RECORDED INTELLIGENCE	TIME (GMT)	REMARKS
LIN 712	LIN 362	SEVEN ONE TWO, FROM, ER, THREE SIX TWO. DO YOU READ?	1103	
		I DON'T THINK HE'S CALLED. WE HAVEN'T GOT SEVEN ONE TWO, HAVE WE?		Intercom
LIN 362	LONDON AIRWAYS	ER, THREE SIX TWO, THERE'S A SEVEN ONE TWO. HE SHOULD CHECK STRUMBLE AT, ER, ZERO THREE, AND IN POINT OF FACT HE HASN'T CALLED US YET		
LONDON AIRWAYS	LIN 362	ER, ROGER, THAT'S THE, ER, CALL-SIGN WE THOUGHT WE HEARD, OSCAR MIKE. HE'S MOST LIKELY TO BE SEVEN ONE TWO		
LIN 362	LONDON AIRWAYS	ROGER, YOU RECKON HIS, ER, OTHER CALL-SIGN IS OSCAR MIKE, DO YOU?		
LONDON AIRWAYS	LIN 362	ER, THAT'S AFFIRMATIVE		
LIN 362	LONDON AIRWAYS	THANK YOU		
LONDON AIRWAYS	TWA 705	TWA. SEVEN OH FIVE OUT OF THREE FOR FOUR		
TWA 705	LONDON	ROGER, SEVEN OH FIVE, CLIMB TO EIGHT ZERO INITIALLY		
LONDON RADAR	TWA 705	— K, RE-CLEARED TO EIGHT ZERO. THANK YOU		

TO	FROM	RECORDED INTELLIGENCE	TIME (GMT)	REMARKS
		FIVE OH SIX ABEAM WOODLEY AND OVER		Intercom
BOA 506	LONDON AIRWAYS	FIVE OH SIX ??? ??? ??? ???		(Poor) modulation) ?? unreadable.
BOA 506	LONDON RADAR	ER FIVE OH SIX, RADAR. CONTINUE ON COURSE TO GARSTON WITH LONDON ONE ONE NINE DECIMAL TWO		
LONDON RADAR	BOA 506	ONE ONE NINE TWO	1104	
		YOU DIDN'T GO OUT D		Intercom
LIN 712	LONDON AIRWAYS	AER LINGUS SEVEN ONE TWO, ER — AER LINGUS SEVEN ONE TWO, LONDON, ONE THREE ONE DECIMAL TWO. YOU ON THE FREQUENCY?		First part very poorly modulated.
LONDON AIRWAYS	CAM 4097	LONDON AIRWAYS, CAMBRIAN FOUR ZERO NINE SEVEN		
CAM 4097	LONDON AIRWAYS	FOUR ZERO NINE SEVEN, LONDON		
LONDON AIRWAYS	CAM 4097	FOUR ZERO NINE SEVEN AIRBORNE AT, ER, FIVE EIGHT. CLIMBING TO SIX ZERO ESTIMATING BERRY HEAD THREE ONE		
CAM 4097	LONDON AIRWAYS	ROGER, IS THAT BERRY HEAD AT THIRTY-ONE ?	1105	

Appendix 1

TO	FROM	RECORDED INTELLIGENCE	TIME (GMT)	REMARKS
LONDON AIRWAYS	CAM 4097	ER, AFFIRMATIVE, FOUR ZERO NINE SEVEN		
CAM 4097	LONDON AIRWAYS	ROGER, CLEARED, ER, CLIMBING, ER, ON AMBER TWENTY-FIVE TO FLIGHT LEVEL SIX ZERO. ER, FURTHER CLIMB TO SEVEN ZERO LATER		
LONDON AIRWAYS	CAM 4097	FOUR ZERO NINE SEVEN, UNDERSTOOD		
LONDON RADAR	TWA 705	TWA SEVEN OH FIVE OUT OF SEVEN FOR EIGHT		
		WHO WAS THAT D		Intercom
LONDON RADAR	TWA 705	TWA SEVEN OH FIVE OUT OF SEVEN FOR EIGHT		
TWA 705	LONDON RADAR	ROGER, SEVEN OH FIVE. CONTINUE THE CLIMB TO FLIGHT LEVEL TWO EIGHT ZERO NOW		
LONDON RADAR	TWA 705	OK THANK YOU UNRESTRICTED NOW TO TWO EIGHT OH	1106	Channel Quiet
		IF YOU HAVEN'T DONE IT ALREADY YOU MIGHT SUGGEST TO AER LINGUS, THE COMPANY FREQUENCY, SEE IF THEY'VE GOT ANY TRACE OF THIS AIRCRAFT .		Intercom
		STANDBY, RADAR, PLEASE		Intercom

TO	FROM	RECORDED INTELLIGENCE	TIME (GMT)	REMARKS
LONDON AIRWAYS	LIN 362	LONDON AIRWAYS, AER LINGUS THREE SIX TWO BY STRUMBLE ZERO SIX. LEVEL ONE THREE ZERO. AMMANFORD ONE FIVE, BRECON NEXT.	1107	

TRANSCRIPTION FROM THE TAPE RECORDING OF RADIO TRANSMISSIONS BY CORK APPROACH CONTROL AT 11.20 GMT ON 24 MARCH 1968

At 11.20 hours three transmissions were made by Cork Approach in a final attempt to contact EI-AOM. One of these was made on the international distress frequency of 121.5 MHz. No replies were received, and we now know that the aircraft had already struck the sea at this time. There was mounting anxiety and tension at that ground station, evidenced by the fact that the first call, intended to be made on 121.5 MHz, was in fact initially transmitted in error on 119.3

1120	APP	EI712	(On 119.3) Aer Lingus 712. 712, Cork Approach calling on 121.5 … disregard. (No reply)
1120	APP	EI712	Aer Lingus 712. 712, Cork Approach calling 121.5. Do you read? (No reply)
1121	APP	EI712	Aer Lingus 712. 712 Cork Approach calling 119.3. (No reply)

TRANSCRIPT OF RECORDING OF THE TELEPHONE LINE BETWEEN SHANNON AREA CONTROL AND LONDON AIRWAYS ON 24 MARCH 1968

Period: 10.36 to 10.44 GMT

This transcript was also cut short; it should have extended to 11.25 hours, the time when a 'Full Alert' was called. This made it impossible to verify the logs and reports made by the London and Shannon staff, and the conversations which ensued when London advised Shannon of the distress call which had just been intercepted at 10.58 hours.

Exp'Air attempted to secure the London tape with no success.

Time	From	To	Text
1036	Shannon	London	Hello One, estimate Aer Lingus 712
	London	Shannon	On who? Aer Lingus 712? I have got 172. Is this 712? That's Cork to London?
	Shannon	London	Cork to London. That's right
	London	Shannon	It's 712, not 172?
	Shannon	London	Yes, 712
	London	Shannon	Okay
	Shannon	London	712 is Flight Level 170, and he is Strumble at 1107.
	London	Shannon	OK. Thank you
1038:20	Shannon	London	Hello, Sector 6. Have you any objections to the Irish 712 routing direct from Cork to Strumble?
1039	London	Shannon	None at all.
1042	London	Shannon	A westbound estimate on Speedbird 501 …
	Shannon	London	Yes …
	London	Shannon	501 estimate Strumble 1106, 310, 465 Knots London. Green One, upper Blue 10. Kennedy via Cork.

Time	From	To	Text
	Shannon	London	310 is the Level?
	London	Shannon	Yes
1043	Shannon	London	Hello Six, a revision on Aer Lingus 712. He's estimating Strumble at 1103, and he is routing Cork direct to Strumble and I've got an estimate for you as well.
	London	Shannon	Okay
1044	Shannon	London	It's from Dublin actually. It's Aer Lingus 362.
	London	Shannon	Stand by. What was the other one?
	London	Shannon	It's Aer Lingus 362, a Viscount. Strumble 1107, Level 130, 267 knots, Dublin to Bristol. Okay, and the Aer Lingus 712 is routing direct to Strumble. Is that OK?
	Shannon	London	Yes, that's all right.
	Shannon	London	Okay, thank you.

Appendix 2

A. LIST OF PITCH TRIM ACCIDENTS

The schedule which follows sets out a brief description of nine incidents which involved limitation of pitch control owing to trim problems. In five of the events the aircraft crashed, killing all on board.

Accident List	Pitch Trim Setting
2 February 1963 Northwest 720 ex-Miami. Steep dive from 17,500 ft. Captain believed aircraft was about to stall, and he trimmed nose-down. Aerodynamic forces in dive prevented re-trimming to pitch up i.e. stalled jackscrews.	Wreckage showed trim was positioned within 3/32 inch of the nose-down mechanical stop.
29 November 1963 Trans-Canada DC-8 ex-Montreal. Dived during climb. All 118 on board killed.	Trim set at 1.65 to 2 degrees nose-down. Possible pitch trim compensator failure. Also possible icing on pitot head caused low airspeed reading, or gyro horizon was faulty.
Beech 99 Nosed over into a dive while at cruise altitude. Did not recover.	Horizontal stab trim 'ran away' to the full nose-down position.

Boeing 727 Pilot tried to compensate for rough air by using up-and-down trim. Recovered from dive ex-28,000 feet at 400 feet above ground. Aircraft shot up again due to excessive corrective trim. Final recovery at higher altitude.

Non-fatal incident. Trim setting inputs excessive in both directions.

3 June 1962 Air France 707 ex-Orly. Servo trim motor failed on stabiliser. 130 dead. Not very relevant to EI-AOM because it occurred during take-off.

2 units nose-down

12 July 1963 United 720 ex-San Francisco. Dive and recovery. Not very relevant as this was a high-altitude stall.

Coarse stabiliser trim inputs, with no result. Saved by idle power and speed brakes.

19 March 2001 Comair Brasilia ex-Nassau to Florida. Encountered unexpected ice at 17,000 feet. Airspeed decreased from 200 to 180 knots and autopilot began trimming nose-up. Speed fell to 140 knots at full nose-up trim. Autopilot disconnected. Roll excursion through 360 deg. to right. Crew recovered aircraft at 10,000 ft. 'Substantial' damage to tailplanes/elevators.

Some similarities to EI-AOM i.e. altitude, cruise mode, something unexpected. Viscounts known to be vulnerable to elevator flow separation in moderate ice. (SE-FOZ, N242V)

19 March 2001 Cessna 560 Citation Fan Jet Executive, at 30,000 feet. Pitch control became 'sluggish' and deteriorated. Pilot descended below 10,000 ft, where the controls returned to normal. He made a precautionary landing at Orlando.

Aircraft had been parked overnight at West Palm Beach ramp during heavy rain. After landing, the belly bilge was found to contain a lot of water. Freezing level was 12,000 ft. The ice had covered the control cables and pulleys of the elevator and trim.

31 January 2000 Alaska Airlines MD-83. Above the Pacific Ocean, off California. Aircraft plunged from altitude, killing all 88 on board. US Navy recovered much wreckage from great depth, including the stabiliser jackscrew and its gimbal nut.

Pilot reported problems with pitch trim while at cruise altitude. During a C-5 maintenance check it was found that 'end-play on gimbal nut was at maximum allowable'. Nut not replaced. No grease on jackscrew.

B. FIRST SCHEDULE OF NEW WRECKAGE
(recovered in County Wexford during October 2000)

Memoranda via télécopie:
TO: Admiral Yves Lemercier or Capt. Manuel Pech
FROM: Capt. Mike Reynolds, Ireland.
        23 October 2000
Re: Les nouveaux débris découverts

As arranged by telephone with Manuel Pech, I transmit herewith a schedule of the new wreckage traced up to 23 October 2000.

All pieces will be photographed today with their identification tags, and I will send you those photos when they are processed, together with the original confirmation of these télécopie pages. The items are kept in safe custody, and I await your instructions regarding the next step, or where to send them.

I spoke to a retired Coxswain from the Rosslare Lifeboat crew, who is very familiar with the flow of currents in the Tuskar Rock region. His name is Fergus Wickham. He affirms that the prevailing flow is towards the north-west on a rising tide, and on a reciprocal track heading south-east on an ebb tide. His comprehensive local knowledge indicates that most flotsam and sea bed movements, from the Tuskar Rock area, finish up ashore much further north, near Cahore Point or in the regions around Blackwater and Curraghcloe. He feels it would be prudent to make inquiries in that geographical area in an attempt to trace other souvenir hunters who may still have pieces of EI-AOM.

At the request by telephone from Manuel Pech I have commenced detailed inquiries concerning the movements of Greenland White-Fronted Geese. There are also other migratory breeds which could be relevant to your inquiries, and I propose to take a close look at the Whooper Swans and Bewick's Swans.

Regards,

Mike

'A' This appears to be a small outer skin section, and it bears the paint scheme and pale green colour used by Aer Lingus in 1968. It is in remarkably good condition. There has been very little abrasion to the paint by movement over the sea bed, and it must have reached the beach soon after the crash. 400 mm x 210 mm. Thickness: 0.7 mm.

The horizontal solid-green pinstripes may help to identify its original location.

'B' 490 mm x 395 mm. Thickness: 1.9 mm. This piece is in mint condition, and there are many clues to identify its original function. There is a fold running full width, but this appears to be at exactly 90 degrees to the lengthwise edge, and may not be a result of the impact. There is a small thin 70 mm x 60 mm aluminium label bonded to the surface.

Even with the naked eye it is possible to read the legend on it, spaced exactly as follows:

'1 7 5226 '
74

The four left-hand figures might be a 'safe life' date or similar. (1 July 1974?)

The numbers are not in symmetric lines, and were obviously created by a hand-held punch and hammer. Rolls-Royce Dart 510A engines, as fitted to EI-AOM in the 1960s, bore Manufacture Serial Numbers of four digits, all starting with the figure 5. The number 5226 would fit that category. However, if this was to be viewed by your experts as an engine number, it does not match any engine which the Aer Lingus maintenance records, or the 1970 investigation team, stated were fitted to EI-AOM on the crash date. The closest number relates to Engine No. 2, which was '5217'. Perhaps it has no connection with engine numbers at all, or it is a post-build modification.

'C' 350 mm x 135 mm. Thickness: 1 mm. This curved section spent some time in the sea, but is relatively unscathed. The close proximity of the rivet holes to each other (15 mm centres gap for the smaller rivets; 35 mm centres gap for the larger rivets) would seem to indicate that this piece derives from a critical area of the aircraft, and was reinforced against failure. A crack which has propagated, and was stopped by another rivet hole, or a designed arrester hole, may have been caused by the impact forces. No doubt your experts can tell.

'D' Thickness: 0.9 to 1 mm. Probably triangular originally. It has two equilateral sides of about 300 mm each, with a hypotenuse of a little over 400 mm. Three holes are drilled near one edge (not the hypotenuse), starting near the 90 degree corner, and spaced at about 110 mm centres. On the other side, which is at right-angle to the drilled side, a larger hole is drilled mid-way near the edge. Incredibly, this still has its rubber grommet intact in place. This same side has a wide tab extension which still retains a '+' shaped black anti-vibration mount. There is a violent tear from the 90 degree corner to the centre of the triangle.

'E' This is an alloy extrusion piece, about 580 mm long. It is of right-angle cross-section, with an additional channel which could have retained a seal or something similar.

It has fractured at both ends, each time at a rivet hole. There are 15 such rivet holes, if we include the fractured ends. The thickness of the flat edge on the extrusion is about 1.8 mm and there appears to be a residue of some type of insulating material bonded to it.

It does not appear to have failed in tension, but shows signs of shear or bending forces. The forces acted in opposite directions at the two respective fracture points.

'F' About 160 mm x 160 mm. Thickness: 1 mm. A small tab, about 60 mm x 35 mm, now lies flat, but could have been at right angle, judging by a flexing crease at the extension joint. This tab has a 6 mm hole drilled off-centre.

At the edges there remain five fixings which have fold-over rectangular washers. It is possible that part of the fixings is of ferrous material, as there is evidence of oxidisation.

'G' This rectangular piece is about 265 mm x 180 mm, and it is 1.5 mm thick. A crease along the centre appears to be exactly parallel to the edges, and the original may have been at 90 degrees in an L-shape cross-section. A further 90 degree bend of 20 mm at the edge material has been carried out at manufacture, probably to aid rigidity. The shape is now a flattened presentation.

'H' This is an irregular shaped piece of 1 mm plate. It measures about 570 mm x 360 mm. There are some violent tears in it, and no identifying features. It really needs an expert eye from a professional 'tin-kicker'.

'J' This was probably a circular item, with a diameter of about 19 mm.

It is about 0.6 mm thick, and there would have been eight equidistant holes drilled near the perimeter, four of which can be seen. The wide spacing of the fixing holes, and the thin material, would seem to indicate that this could have been something like a small inspection panel or of similar function.

'K' Similar to 'H' above, except that it is slightly thicker at 1.2 mm. It has been torn violently from its original location.

'L' This small piece measures about 200 mm x 80 mm and is about 1 mm thick. Of the six rivet holes, five of them still have the rivets in place.

'M' Appears to have been trawled up by a fishing boat. It still has part of the trawl net entwined around the end. It is 1.2 mm thick and measures about 170 mm x 80 mm.

'N' It is unlikely that this piece has any story to tell. About 150 mm x 100 mm, it has suffered from immersion, and was originally about 0.6 mm thick.

'P' The writer has an instinctive feeling that this piece is not from EI-AOM. I may be wrong. However, I have included it for examination because it is fabricated from aluminium, or from an alloy. It was found close to some other items, on the beach adjacent to Greenore Point where the identified section of the spring tab from the portside elevator was found. It measures 1,230 mm x 150 mm, and is 1.5 mm thick.

This list is effective up to, and including, 23 October 2000. Any further items recovered will be listed separately.

C. MEMO TO EXP'AIR, DRAWING ATTENTION TO CLIMB PERFORMANCE ANOMALY

TO: Admiral Yves Lemercier/Capt. Manuel Pech
FROM: Mike Reynolds, Ireland
        6 November 2000
Re: Australian accidents, etc.

Further to our lengthy brainstorming 'think-tank' meeting at Hunter's Hotel, Ashford, on Saturday, I now enclose as promised the complete Final Report on Viscount VH-TVC, which I have obtained from the Mitchell Library in Sydney through an old colleague. I also enclose a synopsis of the *Probable Cause* for two other Australian Viscounts, VH-RMI and VH-RMQ.

Yves did mention to me that he was looking at any possibility of marine salt exposure, during the KLM ownership of EI-AOM. I enclose a sample report of an accident resulting from contamination in a salt environment. The corroded elevator control cable simply snapped, and a pulley was damaged. (N43SP–Canada)

Out of curiosity, I sketched a graph of the climb profile of EI-AOM, which I enclose (Vertical scale = *altitude*; Horizontal scale = *time in minutes* from take-off).

The figures have been derived from Air Traffic Control taped records at Cork, Shannon and London. Two observations are possible, if the ATC times, and the en route altimeter readings reported by radio from EI-AOM, are accurate.

Lacking a Flight Data Recorder or Cockpit Voice Recorder, it is still possible to use other sources, however crude and unpolished they may be, to get a rough picture. If your investigation team has access to a line pilot, current or retired, and with high flying hours on Viscounts, he might add some refinement to the data, and to its interpretation:

(i)   The flight was airborne at 1032 hours. Confirmation of that time was made in a radio call from Cork Tower to the aircraft at 1033 hours, i.e. '*712 was airborne at 32...contact Approach 119.3*'

By 1036 hours, EI-AOM had reached 6,000 feet, a climb rate of 1,500 feet per minute. Between 1036 and 1040 hours there appears to be a dramatic reduction in the rate of climb. In those four minutes he only appears to have gained a total of 1,500 ft, from 6,000 ft up to 7,500 ft, which translates to 375 fpm. This is well below the usual climb performance of a Viscount (25% of normal), although it might be related to re-trimming from takeoff power to climb power. However, this is very unlikely, as takeoff power would have been reduced long before the radio call at 1036 hours (Cork transcript) i.e. *'Six zero…climbing to one seven zero'*. At 1040 hours (Shannon transcript) the crew called *' … by Youghal at 7,500'* (change to Shannon frequency was at 1039:45).

The next report was *'passing 9,000'* at 1041 hours + 20 secs, indicating that they were once again climbing at a more realistic rate, required to reach 17,000 ft before they arrived at the change-over control zone boundary between Shannon and London.

Is it possible that for four minutes they had been 'feeling out' a trim problem, or sticky control runs? Had a bird damaged a tailplane? Was any ice accretion possible? *'Moderate icing'* was after-cast on that day in the Strumble region between 6,000 ft and 13,000 ft, with *'light icing'* at 17,000 ft. Perhaps a developing problem, not yet sufficiently worrying to make a descriptive radio call, or a return to Cork?

(ii) It is only when the climb is shown in the form of a graph, and the known radioed 'upset' time is highlighted (*'Twelve thousand feet, descending, spinning rapidly'*, transmitted at 1058 hours + 10 seconds), that the visual presentation shouts out loudly for attention, asking if any control inputs had just occurred at about 1057 hours. The call *'Level at 170'* came at 1051 hours + 48 seconds, from which it can be deduced that EI-AOM flew in normal cruise mode for about five minutes at 17,000 ft. The first radio call hinting at an existing problem was intercepted by London Radar at 1058 hours + 2 secs. It used non-standard text. The graph seems to be making a statement to remind us that the transition from climb to cruise level would have called for forward pressure on the control column to decrease the angle-of-attack, re-trim the elevators, and set cruise power. It was very shortly afterwards that the fatal upset occurred. When one looks at the graph it just seems to say that it is too much of a coincidence that the spin was initiated just after the top of the climb. Up to that point the flight had proceeded normally for 25 minutes, *as far as we know*. I also enclose extra synopses of two other Viscount accidents, where undetected ice accretion on the tailplanes/elevators caused flow separation and stall. Both aircraft were also 800 Series types like EI-AOM (SE-FOZ and N242V).

Coincident with the contents of (ii) above, the *Probable Cause* for N242V is given as *'loss of pitch control, in conjunction with a specific airspeed and specific configuration'*. Thought-provoking?

Regards,

Mike

D. IDENTIFICATION OF MIGRATORY TRACKS OF SWANS AND GEESE, ON POTENTIAL COLLISION COURSES WITH EI-AOM AT ALTITUDE AND IN THE CLIMB

Memo to Exp'Air: Migratory Geese and Swans

I consulted the leading Irish expert on this subject. I also sought a second opinion from another specialist, to confirm the information.

The acknowledged authority is Oscar Merne, Head of Bird Research at Dúchas (the Irish Heritage Service), which is a subsidiary of the Irish Government's Department of Arts, Culture and the Gaeltacht. Mr Merne has published papers in international ornithological journals concerning the migratory flight patterns of the birds in question. He has tracked them at various altitudes, and has used light aircraft in his research. The second expert is Richard Nairn, of Natura Environment Consultancy in Wicklow town. For many years he was National Director of the Irish Wildbird Conservancy.

ERRORS IN THE 1970 REPORT

Before writing any details, I should say at the outset that both of these experts are emphatic that parts of the 1970 Report are not accurate.

I showed Sec. 2.1.1.4. [sub-section (vi)] to Mr Nairn. It reads:

'and expert opinion considers that owing to the good weather that prevailed prior to March 24, most if not all of the large birds (geese) would have left.'

Mr Merne and Mr Nairn both state that no expert would ever make such a statement. The weather in Ireland has no effect on the departure date. This has always occurred in April since records began. The geese must wait for the ice cap in Greenland to commence thawing, and provide a food source. They never leave their rich feeding grounds in Ireland to travel early to Greenland, simply to starve to death there on the ice cap.

The table of official recorded departure times and dates from Wexford for the period 1969–1975 is enclosed. This was the nearest to 1968 which I could trace in the time available to me.

The same sub-section of the report also contains another statement, with relevance to the crash time of about 1100 hours GMT (noon local time):

'and migration rarely takes place in daytime, especially round about mid-day'.

This is equally untrue. I enclose a copy of a paper published by Oscar Merne, entitled *Irish Bird Report 1974*, which includes the records of migratory bird movements for 1969–1975 from the Wexford Sloblands. The table on p. 64 shows that in 1969, one year after the crash, 62% of the geese left on 29 April, and 26% of the flocks departed on 30 April. If you now refer to p. 65 you will see that a *peak* movement occurs between 1000 hours and 1100 hours, and very few birds fly after sunset. There are official records of a similar nature dating back to earlier centuries, and one definitive work is titled *The Migration of Birds as observed at Irish Lighthouses and Lightships*, which includes Tuskar Rock light-house. It was compiled in 1899 by Richard M. Barrington, MA, LLB, FLS, and Mr Nairn has a first edition.

Description of the Wexford Sloblands

With some luck I sourced a back-copy of the magazine *Ireland*, published by the Irish Tourist Board. It is dated January 1996, and on pages 26–31 there is a detailed description of the Wexford Slobs and Harbour showing flock numbers, species and photos.

This magazine, enclosed herewith, also confirms mid-April as the departure date. The author, Christopher J. Wilson, is the one man on earth who can say that with some certainty. He is the Warden of Wexford Wildfowl Reserve. About 5,000 to 7,000 of the Greenland White-Fronted Goose species spend winter on the Wexford Slobs.

Other Wetlands on the Flight Path of EI-AOM

I enclose maps of other wetlands near the flight path, together with a legend illustrating the flock numbers of birds in each area. They commence in the region of Cork Airport and continue east along the climb-out from Cork Airport, and the subsequent climb from Youghal en route to Strumble Head. Separate detailed maps of these individual locations are also enclosed.

How high?

During their feeding season within Ireland, flocks of swans or geese travel at relatively low altitudes, sometimes only moving from one local feeding ground to another. These short flights are made below 2,000 feet.

I was amazed to discover from Oscar Merne that geese often fly at an altitude of 20,000 feet on their journey to Greenland. The temperature at that height is well below zero, and oxygen is low. The altitude record for Irish migratory birds was set by a flock of Whooper Swans at 26,400 feet above the Outer Hebrides, inbound for Ireland from Iceland. Although he has studied them all his life, Oscar has no idea how they achieve these feats of flight. They have no 'hot wing' or de-icer boots, and they lack oxygen masks. These birds have a unique breathing system whereby the ram-air is forced through three pairs of air sacs in a single direction. This method of oxygen extraction is much more efficient than the bellows lung system employed by mammals. They just plod on, burning the last of their fat reserves.

Rate of climb/Angle of climb/Airspeeds

In 1970 and 1973, Oscar Merne tracked the geese leaving the Wexford Slobs.

He used a Beagle Pup aircraft, which has a low stalling speed. A comprehensive description of these experiments is included in the document enclosed herewith. The airfield is 4 kilometres north-west of the birds' take-off point. At several miles north of the airfield, some birds had levelled off between 1,200 and 1,600 feet, while others were *still climbing* at 2,200 feet. The angle of climb for geese is 20–25 degrees, and their airspeed is 38–39 knots.

The Bewick's Swans

The 1970 Report failed to examine swan migrations. Yet flocks of Bewick's Swans crossed the track of Flight 712 during the week of the crash, between County Wexford and an en route feeding stop at Slimbridge, near the River Severn.

These journeys occur every year between mid-February and the end of March, when the swans are returning to their breeding grounds in Arctic Russia and Siberia (extract from *Ireland's Wetlands and their Birds*, pp. 144/145, compiled by Clive Hutchinson between 1971 and 1975 for Irish Wildbird Conservancy, with material supplied by Oscar Merne). The European wintering population is about 9,000 birds.

It is known that some well-fed flocks leaving distant Shannon areas and Galway turloughs may overshoot Slimbridge. Instead, they fly non-stop to the east coast of England, touching down at Welney, on the River Ouse washes. Others fly direct to Denmark. These birds can easily reach 17,000 feet, arising from the higher rate of climb used for such long-haul journeys.

Regards,

Mike

Appendix 3

PART A

CONTROLLED DEVIATION FROM FLIGHT PLAN?

In this section, the international team examines the possibility that the pilots deliberately deviated from the flight plan, and lied. If the crew did so, it would have been necessary to make two 'pop-up' climbs from low level flight at 1051 and 1057 hours to transmit spurious messages that they were at 17,000 feet. Some measure of altitude is required to gain line of sight between an aircraft antenna and the aerial of a ground station for VHF transmissions. Crews were aware that signals transmitted at altitudes below 3,000 feet, when east of the hills which lie south-east of Shannon, would not be read. NOTE: The mother tongue of the authors of the verbatim analyses is French. Hence quaint constructions of English sentences appear in the texts.

5.4.3 Scenario 'As per Witnesses/Deviation from the Flight Plan'

Since it is difficult to imagine that the Shannon ATC introduced a distortion between the original recording and the R/T communications transcript, the first assumption is to consider that the crew, deliberately, decided to divert from their flight plan and to report wrong positions at regular timing.

5.4.3.1 Flight Reconstruction

Based on this assumption, the low altitude flight observed by several witnesses is not the consequence of a damage suffered by the Viscount, but the execution of the deliberate will of the Captain. Explainable reasons: touristic or familial flight over a place or a person well known by him, or deviating flight at the request of a passenger (for instance, an American passenger may have asked to fly over the Kennedys' house).

It is to be noted that every pilot knew that, when flying at low altitude (lower than 2 to 3,000 feet) in a zone located East of the hills South-East of Shannon, the VHF radio waves propagation being poor, the transmissions between the aircraft and Shannon ATC could not be usually established.

It is to be noted also that the Viscount was observed after its first dive, when flying over Old Parish, at low altitude. Then, it was continuously observed from Tramore to Brownstown Head, Tory Hill, Ballykelly and Fethard area. Along this track, it was observed above 2,000 to 3,000 feet only in the vicinity of the Kennedy Arboretum.

If, in order to communicate with Shannon ATC, the Captain had to climb the aircraft in a pop-up manoeuvre at the minutes 51 and 57, this manoeuvre could have taken place only:

a) Between Old Parish and Tramore, when flying over the sea, out of the sight of any witness.
b) In the vicinity of the Kennedy Arboretum, where the Viscount was observed climbing and then descending.
c) Between Fethard and Tuskar Rock, when flying over the sea, out of the sight of any witness.

1st supposition: The Viscount was over Kennedy Arboretum at 51.

An argument in favour of this scenario is that, since the Viscount did not crash when flying over the ground, the crew had the control of the aircraft; and since the Viscount avoided (for example) the steeple of the Ballykelly church and then headed just between the hills, this meant that the crew had full control of the aircraft.

If the crew had the full control of the aircraft after the descent observed over Kennedy Arboretum, this means that the Captain had gained altitude for his radioing message, then descended and continued his 'diverted' flight.

Those observations drive to the assumption that the Viscount should have flown over Kennedy Arboretum at mn 51.

It is to be noted that the max. normal operating speed of the Viscount is 230 kts (air speed) and that the speed not to exceed (VNE) is 270 kts.

In this case, if the Captain initiated the descent at 42, flew over Old Parish for 1 or 2 mn, then, direct to Tramore, and according to the reconstructed track at low altitude to Brownstown Head and Tory Hill, the average ground speed should have been 365 kts **which is impossible**.

Consequently, the Viscount could not be over the Kennedy Arboretum at mn 51.

2nd supposition: The Viscount was over Kennedy Arboretum at mn 58.

Then, the first pop-up should have taken place at mn 51, out of the sight of any witness, somewhere over the sea between Old Parish and Tramore.

Let us suppose that it was quite at the end of the flight leg over the sea (even if this is in a certain way contradicted by a witness who saw the Viscount appearing at very low altitude behind Newton village).

In this case the average ground speed between Old Parish and Tramore should be 215 kts, which is quite realistic.

From Tramore to Tory Hill at low altitude, and climbing from Tory Hill, in such a way that the Viscount was above 3,000 feet at 57, and above 5,000 feet at 58, the average ground speed is around 250 kts, which is slightly high, but acceptable, in particular if the Captain was in a hurry to respect his ETA Strumble (min 03), which in any case, could not be respected.

The damaging initial event should then occur above the Kennedy Arboretum, and the last part of the flight (positioning, timing, and degradation process) should have been the same as in the above described scenario (as per witnesses/disabled flight).

The argument related to the Viscount handling easiness at Ballykelly is no longer valid.

Consequently, **the track reconstruction** should be **described as follows** [in local time]:

11.32 h Take off from Cork.

11.42 h After having established the R/T liaison with Shannon, and having given the ETA Strumble, beginning of the deviation from the flight plan. Rapid descent and flight at low altitude over Old Parish, then to Tramore.

11.51 h Pop-up over the sea to transmit the message 'Level at 170'.

11.57 h When passing 3,000 feet, climbing, heading towards the Saltees and Strumble, reporting as if at the FIR boundary.

11.58 h While climbing, above 5,000 feet, a sudden event damages the tail of the Viscount, thus resulting in a spin turning right, which was observed from Tory Hill.

Distress message: 'EI-AOM with you ...' relayed to London ATC by two aircraft in flight, but also recorded on London tape.

Then, flight similar to what has been described in the here-above scenario 'disabled flight'.

5.4.3.2 Assessment

In order to determine the level of probability of occurrence of such a scenario, each step of the 'deviation' process is to be analysed:

- Filing up of an IFR flight plan
- Decision to divert from the flight plan
- Preparation for executing the diversion
- Diversion execution.

5.4.3.2.1 Filing up of an IFR Flight Plan

It may be necessary to know what an IFR flight plan is.

A flight plan is a pseudo-contract between the Captain and the ATS: the ATS commits itself to inform the Captain for preventing any collision, managing horizontal and vertical separations, for assuring a safe take-off, climbing, en route flight, descending and landing inside the complex traffic which exists around the major airports; and for providing any necessary help in case of in-flight unexpected event.

On the other side, the Captain commits himself to follow at the best the routing instructions, fixed in the flight plan, to report to the ATS when necessary and to react adequately to the information given by the various ATCs. In all cases, the Captain remains responsible for assuring the prevention of collision and the safety of his environment.

In order to assure these commitments, strict procedures have been implemented. A 'flight plan' format is filled in by the crew before take-off.

Since it is a flight of public transport, the rule is that the flight plan is IFR, which means that the maximum services (as listed here above) are provided by the ATC to the crew.

But it was possible, in the late sixties, to request on those parts of the flight path, as decided by the Captain, to fly under VFR conditions. In that case, the ATC provide traffic announcement and the Captain assumes the total responsibility of the flight safety, towards his passengers and toward the external world.

When the flight plan is filled in, the ATC who has received it, phones and faxes it to the other concerned ATC.

The crew has to ask the ATC for the clearance before starting up which is given when the traffic density allows for.

The crew then asks the flight clearance, before take-off. The clearance is given by the ATC, eventually with some modifications necessitated by the traffic situation. The crew's read-back of the clearance is compulsory.

Whilst the flight is going on, the ATC provides the crew with any relevant information, and the crew reports on the flight progress and possible events.

Some specific procedures, very strict, are implemented

between the different ATCs to follow the flight, without error or omission. One of these procedures, at the time, was the 'strip', which allowed a controller to get a clear situation of the flight he had under control. The basic check was to control that the information written on the strip was according first to the flight planning, and secondly to the contents of the crew reporting messages.

One of the major services provided to the crew by the ATS was an efficient guidance when entering the crowded zones around the major airports.

Consequently, these zones were very soon equipped with radars, assuring a positive control of the aircraft, being usually (it was the case of EI-AOM) fitted with a transponder, able to give the identity of the 'transponding' aircraft.

At the time, the radar coverage between the zones over the large airports was not complete; for instance, the radar coverage between Cork and London was nil from Cork to East Strumble.

Consequently, when flying under an IFR flight plan from Cork to London, two reporting points were of particular importance: the FIR boundary, when the control responsibility of the aircraft switched from the Irish ATS to the British ATS, and Strumble, from where London ATC had to calculate the best flight elements to manage the best trajectory down to the landing.

The ETA at the FIR boundary was not a key factor; the ETA Strumble was for London AWYS a key information: as such, Strumble Head was VOR/DME/Beacon equipped for accurate reporting.

On that Sunday morning, it can be observed that the IFR flight plan was written by the F 712 co-pilot, without any reference to a possible VFR leg. It was a 'scheduled flight', under a standard and repetitive flight plan.

At that instant, the Captain was presumably not aware that he should have later to take a decision about a possible diversion from the flight plan; if not, he should have filed up the flight plan by himself, and should have warned the controller, either in a written form (mixed VFR/IFR in the flight plan); or in an oral procedure which was sometimes used at that time, according to the controllers interviewed.

5.4.3.2.2 Decision to Divert from the Flight Plan

If this decision was a 'last minute' decision, it could have been taken up to the minute 42, when a witness saw the Viscount diving.

However, it may be noticed that, even after the take-off, some statutory procedures existed, allowing the Captain to divert from his IFR flight plan. He could have asked for a 'PLN deviation'; or for a VFR clearance on a sequence of the IFR flight plan adequately modified; or for a cancellation of his IFR flight plan, since he could later on deposit in flight another IFR flight plan.

One of these procedures would have prevented the Captain from incurring the risk of taking a non-statutory decision: a low altitude deviation may always be observed from the ground by anybody able to report to the relevant authority, and after such a deviation, the Captain may become vulnerable in front of his co-pilot, or other crewmen; he may be blamed by his company; he may suffer higher sanctions, up to temporary interdiction to fly.

In addition, a diversion initiated at flight level 90 or 100, would imply a second climb phase, with the related fuel consumption and consequently the necessity of a justification to be given by the Captain to the Airline.

However, it is observed that, at that time, and with Captains having been combat pilots, such risks were not considered by them determinant.

In addition, the radar coverage was not continuous, and allowed for large deviations without any possible detection. The controller could not know that the aircraft was not where it had to be, nor that it was where it was.

Consequently, without taking into consideration the psychological characteristics of Captain O'Beirne, which were reported to be at the full opposite to such decision, it is possible to suppose that the Captain decided to divert irregularly from his IFR flight plan. It was a Sunday morning, spring time, exceptional good visibility, favourable downwind, flying on his birth place, without any other flight in the vicinity: a Shamrock in his domain …!

5.4.3.2.3 Preparation for Execution of the Diversion

No ETA Strumble had been noted on the flight plan. However, since such flight was daily flown, as soon as the Viscount took off, the controller, by himself, gave the ETA Strumble at 07, normal flight duration between Cork and Strumble.

When the Viscount was proposed by the ATC to fly direct to Strumble without passing over Tuskar, the crew gave an ETA at 03 (4 mn sooner than the normal flight duration). The difference between the distances (Cork–Tuskar–Strumble and Cork direct Strumble) is about 4 nautical miles. The practice in those days was to add a minute if the directed track route was granted. Four minutes seem a bit high unless a higher speed than normal (average ground speed of 251 kts instead of 222 kts) was to be used.

This was said at 41.

If, at that minute, the Captain had the intention to divert, he should have given an ETA later and not sooner.

If he had decided to divert later on, at the very last minute before descent, he should have contacted Shannon to give another ETA Strumble as long as he was at high altitude. This should have taken place before beginning the descent.

5.4.3.2.4 Diversion Execution

The track reconstruction shows that this diversion can be described as follows [local time]:

> 11.42 Descent over Old Paris [Parish]
> 11.42–11.44 Fly low altitude over Old Parish
> 11.44–11.51 Fly low altitude over the sea and Pop-up at 51
> 11.51–11.55 Fly low altitude from South Tramore to Brownstown Head, East Waterford, Tory Hill.

Each of these flight legs is to be cross-checked against the statements of the witnesses.

5.4.3.2.4.1 Descent over Old Parish

A descent with 57 passengers on board is not a fighter exercise. The descent rate should remain within 2 to 3,000 feet/min maximum; the turn rate should also remain rather smooth.

According to a single witness (2.01.2.3), the Viscount showed a steep right turn, then dived almost vertically. The rate of descent would have been so high that the witness made a prayer for the people on board since he was sure the aircraft was to crash.

The fact that the Viscount was not in a smooth descent is confirmed by a lady (2.02.2.1), ex-pilot, ear-witness, who states: 'I have long experience of engine tunes of aircraft and a very keen sense of hearing … I thought that the plane sounded "rather rough".'

Both statements tend to prioritise the assumption that the Viscount was in a disabled condition from the very beginning, i.e. 11.42 [local time].

5.4.3.2.4.2 Flight at Low Altitude over Old Parish

A touristic flight over Old Parish may be considered since:

— *Witness 2.05.1.3* stated: 'I saw an aircraft flying very low … it was circling round … it did that twice.

— *Witness 2.07.1.3*: 'I saw the plane, and it was flying very low over the cliff. It was going in the general direction of Dungarvan …'

These observations may refer to an aircraft flying for touristic purposes, but this type of flight is contradicted by the following statements:

— *2.05.1.3 and 2.06.1.3* saw an aircraft, with propeller Nr 3 'bent'.

It is difficult to imagine a feathering/unfeathering exercise when making this type of touristic diversion.

— *2.07.1.3* '… it appeared to be weaving or going in a zig-zag manner …'

— *2.10.1.1* 'I thought the sound of the engines was peculiar. They seemed to be labouring. My sister Margaret … said to me: "Is that plane making a funny noise?"'

— *2.12.2.3* (ex-teacher) 'The plane was pulling hard and making a dreadful noise.'

Complemented by:

—'… on that day the plane was certainly in trouble passing over this area. I heard an unusual noise which sounded as if the engine was "labouring", and I said to the other members of the household "that plane is in trouble" and they said the sound is unusual.'

Consequently, there is again a tendency to prefer the assumption for a disabled flight over Old Parish.

5.4.3.2.4.3 Flight at Low Altitude over the Sea and Pop-up near Tramore, over the Sea

This leg of the flight was performed out of the sight of any witness.

However, it may be observed that the witness *3.01.2.3* saw the Viscount appearing at very low altitude just North of Newtown Head. If there had been a pop-up at 51, this man would have seen the Viscount, at the top of its trajectory, since the visibility was excellent.

5.4.3.2.4.4 Flight at Low Altitude from South Tramore, Brownstown Head, East Waterford and Tory Hill

This leg of the flight was observed by three witnesses, who could have observed a touristic low altitude flight:

— *3.01.2.3* 'I saw the Viscount crossing the Tramore Bay, at low altitude, slightly climbing steadily …'

— *3.02.2.2* ' I saw, in a glance, a large aeroplane turning left, quite fast, and descending till it disappeared behind the cliffs of Brownstown Head.'

— *4.01.2.3* 'I saw a plane coming from Dungarvan, turning left, leaving Waterford on its left. It was descending, unsteady in roll, down to a height so low that the grass was bent by the air flow … It then turned on the right, by a steep turn, and climbing steadily, headed towards the Saltees.'

However, it may be noted :

— The unsteadiness in roll, at very low altitude, which would be a dangerous crew attitude with 57 pax [passengers] behind, if it was the will of the crew.

— The heading towards the Saltees, and not direct to Tuskar or Strumble, which should have been the normal manoeuvre if occurring at the end of the diversion.

In that scenario, the spin over the Kennedy Arboretum is the initial event of the degradation process of the Viscount.

5.4.3.3 Conclusions

Although an irregular deviation from the flight plan is possible, since:

— There was no positive radar coverage in that area, at low altitude.

— The 'aura' of the Captain, ex-Combat pilot, was imposing enough not to take care of the risks that such a manoeuvre could make them to incur.

— The Viscount was the only aircraft flying in that area, all weather conditions being excellent.

The assessment drives to the conclusion that this scenario is of a very remote possibility, because of:

— The psychological characteristics of the Captain, as reported by several of his relatives and friends.

— The several existing procedures, at that time, to make a 'regular' diversion from the flight plan. If the Captain had decided to satisfy the request of a passenger, for instance, there is no doubt, according to his fellow captains, that he would not have chosen to proceed irregularly.

— The inconsistency of the ETA Strumble correction, if the crew had decided to proceed in that irregular diversion. All along the diversion path, this ETA became more and more unrealistic; and the Captain knew that this was the key information for London to manage at the best his arrival trajectory to London airport.

— The excess of fuel consumption to be justified to the Airline.

— And mainly, this supposition is contradicted by the

witnesses located in Youghal or Old Parish, and raise questions with regard to the statements of the witness at Tory Hill.

Consequently, at this stage, the present study is in a situation quite similar to the one of the 1970 report:

In 1970, the (non) conclusion was: under the assumptions that the transcripts are exact, and that the time of the crash is exact, the air-mobile sighted over Fethard cannot be the Viscount; 'the conclusion that there was such another aircraft in the area is inescapable'.

This sentence fed a 30 years controversy.

Today, the conclusion could be: under the assumption that the crew did not do anything irregular, the conclusion that the transcript of the Shannon radio-comms does not describe the exact R/T is inescapable.

In order to avoid a new 30 years war, a deeper analysis of that conclusion is to be made.

Author's Note:

The 'deeper analysis' referred to by Exp'Air may be seen in Part C .

In the first few lines of the foregoing 'Conclusions', Exp'Air refer to Captain O'Beirne as an 'ex Combat' pilot. From this they infer that the derring-do exploits associated with that role can result in a casual attitude to safety. The captain never flew in combat. Exp'Air probably intended to write 'ex-military', and a misnomer arose within their use of English. The captain did train in the IAC.

PART B

Here Exp'Air examines the proposition that flight 712 sustained an initial upset at about 10.42 hours above Old Parish, and that the aircraft continued to fly in a disabled state for 32 minutes until it crashed.

5.4.2.1.1.1.1 Between Cork and Old Parish

The Viscount took off from Cork, and was instructed to left turn out radial 102, until FL 100. Then, when out of FL 70, Cork Approach authorised a left turn on course for Tuskar. Witness (1.01.1.3) heard, saw and identified the Viscount at short distance to the South of his house, at Aghada Hall (Rostellan). The Viscount was presumably slightly north of its cleared route. The witness saw it, climbing steadily, at normal altitude for an Eastbound plane.

Conclusions: Between Cork and Old Parish area (Dungarvan):
• The Viscount had a route 'as per its flight plan', possibly slightly North of it.
• It was climbing, steadily, at the normal rate of climb.

5.4.2.1.1.1.2 Over Old Parish

One witness (2.01.2.2.), 31 years old at the time of the accident, was standing with a neighbour aged 55, near his home at Scat (North Youghal). He saw the aircraft, and identified it as a Viscount (four engined aircraft). From its position relative to the sun, it can be estimated that the Viscount was at an altitude between FL 90 and FL 100. The aircraft was reported initially as steady, and was seen in this way approximately one minute, when it suddenly turned right, in a very steep turn, and lasting only a few seconds for a 180° turn; in the same time it turned, it also descended. Then after, it spun or spiralled, almost vertically.

After about 30 seconds, the Viscount disappeared behind a hill, clearly identified since a big mast was erected on its top. The witness reported that he then prayed for the people inside the plane, since he was sure that it should crash all at once. From the relative height of the hill and of the witness, it can be estimated that, depending from the distance of the aircraft to the witness, the altitude of the plane when it disappeared behind the hill could be between 1,500 feet and 3,000 feet, thus allowing altitude for a recovery.

When the aircraft was spinning, the witness did not hear anything; it is to be noted that the wind, rather strong in altitude, was blowing from South-West. Accordingly, the witness, being West of the Viscount, could not hear it. The direction of the wind is presumably the reason which explains that two witnesses (2.03.2.1 and 2.04.2.1) in Dungarvan heard a loud bang, with no further bangs.

Then two boys (14 and 13 years old in 1968), witnesses (2.05.1.3) and (2.06.1.3) located in Crobally, saw an 'aeroplane flying very low, ... in a bit from the sea and over the land. It was circling round ... at less than $\frac{1}{2}$ mile from me. It did this about twice ... the plane was silvery and green in colour.'

His brother stated that:

'The plane was facing in the direction of Ardmore when I first saw it. It then turned a bit left towards the sea ... It was flying over the cliff edge ... the top of the plane was silvery and the bottom was dark; around the sides, it was white. There were windows on both sides of it ... I was shown a photograph of a plane similar to the one that crashed and it is like the one I saw yesterday.'

From the same village, Crobally, a housewife (2.07.1.3)

'saw the plane ... over the cliff ... it was going in the general direction of Dungarvan, but at times, it appeared to me it was trying to turn back towards Cork. It appeared to be grey in colour.'

In Ballytrissane, a farmer (2.08.1.1)

'did not see the plane, (but) ... heard the sound of a plane flying very near where I was ... it appeared to be nearly over my head or a little to the South of me, that is towards the sea.'

In Ballymacart, a farm labourer (2.09.1.2) saw

'one plane with four engines ... going towards Cork ... another one ... at the same height, was going towards Mine Head ... it was darkish grey colour.'

In Ballinroad, a farmer and his sister (2.10.1.1 and 2.11.1.1)

'heard the sound of a plane which was passing somewhere to the South ... it could be flying about a mile from here.'

Finally, at Ballintlea, a lady, school teacher (2.12.2.3) well remembers
> 'seeing and hearing the plane ... flying over land at the time having come from Youghal / Ardmore.'

Conclusions : Over the 'Old Parish' area:
A Viscount crossing 9 to 10,000 feet suddenly interrupted its climbing, and dived in a spin (possibly a spiral), right handed, over land or most likely quite a few nautical miles at sea.

It recovered from its dive, and appeared to a witness to be attempting to go back to Cork.

It was seen for two left turns, above the cliffs at Crobally, then heading North-East, seen or heard from Ballytrissane, Ballymacart, Ballinroad and Ballintlea.

During this phase of the flight, it flew at low altitude, at a maximum height of no more than 1,000 to 2,000 feet.

5.4.2.1.1.1.3 Between Old Parish and Tramore, and over Tramore Area

A Waterford crystal blower (3.01.2.3), playing football with his brother near the road of Crobally More saw 'a four engine aircraft, which sounded like the Viscount which I flew one week ago for my wedding trip ... appearing at low altitude, over Newtown, at mid-way between Tramore and Great Newton head. The Viscount crossed Tramore Bay, climbing steadily, at low rate of climb, in such a way that it remained visible above the road hedges. The noise sounded normal, growing when approaching, then disappearing.'

In the same time, from Tramore area, his cousin (3.02.2.2) had a glance on a large aeroplane flying over Brownstown Head, which made a left steep turn, descending and disappearing behind Brownstown Head cliffs.

Conclusions :
From Old Parish to Tramore, the Viscount was not observed. It was presumably low altitude, most of the time over the sea. It then was observed flying low, over Newtown (South

Tramore), crossing Tramore Bay, heading slightly South of Brownstown Head, gaining some hundreds of feet.

Then, suddenly turned left, descending down to nap of the earth, heading North.

5.4.2.1.1.1.4 Between Brownstown Head and the Kennedy Arboretum

A young boy (4.01.2.3), 13 years old, was feeding cattle in his father's field below the wooded area of Tory Hill:

'A large aeroplane approached the field that I was in ... The aeroplane came from the Dungarvan direction, but it turned left after having passed Tramore; it left Waterford on its left. It was ... very low altitude. The plane approached the field as if to land, but suddenly it turned right, and climbed ... I identified a Viscount; I was able to read letters on its side. After the turn, it headed towards the Saltees, but when arriving above of the hills, it suddenly descended and disappeared. I saw it for about 10 minutes, 6 minutes from Tramore to Tory Hill, and 4 minutes after the right turn.'

Conclusions :

From Brownstown Head to Tory Hill, a Viscount was seen heading to Tory Hill, at very low altitude. After a steep turn right, it gained altitude for about 3 to 4 mn, and then, again, suddenly, dived.

5.4.2.1.1.1.5 From Kennedy Arboretum, around Slievecoiltra Hill, to Fethard

A witness (5.01.2), still alive, staying in Ballykelly, stated that:

'While still in the church, attending the Mass, and just before the end of the Mass, all attendants heard a heavy sound, getting louder ... but no one saw anything, at that instant. Later on, just after they went out of the church, maybe 2 to 2 and a half minutes after the sound, while they were on the public place, all of them saw a Viscount, without doubt identified as a Viscount since the witness recognised the colours, the windows and the call-sign letters on the hull. The Viscount was heard for about 2 mn, when it was visible for 1 mn.'

The Viscount appeared from behind the hill (Slievecoitlea), coming from the North-East, heading South-West, very low in altitude. It was so low that the horizon line, defined by the hill was seen above it.

It flew in the exact direction of the steeple of the church, but it avoided it at the very last moment thanks to a left turn.

It then headed South-East, over the Kennedy Arboretum, still low in altitude, but slightly climbing. The Viscount flew so near these witnesses, that they considered the sound as 'enormous'.

South-East from Ballykelly, while praying in a cemetery, two ladies heard the plane passing 'between the cemetery and Campile' (witness 5.02.2.1).

Further South-East, along the road near Ballykeerogebeg (North Campile), a lady (5.03.2.3) cooking in her kitchen was called by her daughter. She went out of her house, and 'saw the aircraft she had heard from inside. It was heading South-East, towards Fethard, at an altitude which could be 1,000 feet.'

Conclusions:

The Viscount, in the area of Kennedy Arboretum, experienced presumably a second dive, which was seen from Tory Hill and heard from Ballykelly. Once again, the crew recovered at very low altitude, flew around Slievecoiltra Hill, over Ballykelly; then headed to Fethard at an altitude around 1,000 feet.

5.4.2.1.1.1.6 Over Fethard Area

Several witnesses heard and saw a plane in that area. (They were all interviewed by the 1968 Investigation Commission. Their statements were interpreted as a possible substantiation for a second aircraft.)

An agricultural labourer (witness 6.01.1.3) living in Saltmills, stated:

'... I heard a noise from what I thought was an average

sized aeroplane coming from the Dunbrody Abbey direction. I looked up and saw ... the plane, ... but it now appeared to be going in the Baginbun Hook Head direction, and seemed to me to be ... apparently descending. I viewed the aeroplane for approximately 30 seconds and I lost sight of it when I considered it to be in a position approximately over Loftus Hall.'

A 12 years old girl (6.02.1.3), staying at Fethard, stated:

'I heard the noise of a plane and my mummy said it was a funny noise. I went out to the garden in front of my home. I saw a plane travelling from the direction of the Protestant Minister's house towards the Saltee Islands. As the plane was travelling, it kept gradually winding away to its right on towards Slade. I kept watching it until it disappeared, and it was still going as I could hear it for a while.'

Two young boys, 12 and 11 years old, playing bows and arrows near their home at Ralph (6.03.1.3 and 6.04.1.3) stated:

(My brother) 'told me to look at a plane that had passed ... I looked at it ... The plane was travelling away from me in a South Easterly direction over Baginbun ... The plane was travelling at medium height.'

His brother confirmed separately the statement in every way, making a firm deposition.

A farmer, living at Loftus Hall, but feeding cattle at Slade at the moment he heard the plane (witness 6.05.1.1), stated:

'I heard the noise of a plane coming from the Hook Head lighthouse direction. In my estimation this plane was between the Baginbun lighthouse and Slade village ... The sound faded away gradually as if the plane was going away from me. I did not look at this plane ... About 3 or 4 minutes later, I heard the noise of a plane back again, the noise seemed to be from between Slade and the Saltee Islands ... This noise was much louder and then sounded as if it was over my head ... The noise from this plane lasted for about 2 mn, and then cut out suddenly. In my opinion, if this was the same plane I heard on both occasions, it definitely altered course and turned back towards the land ...'

A lady (6.06.1.3) was cooking in her kitchen, at Grange Square. She said:

'... I heard the noise of a plane. I went out into the backyard. I saw a plane approaching ... I would say it would be in the direction of the Saltee Islands. I watched for a few minutes ... It was travelling something lower than other planes. Then I went back into the kitchen. About a minute later I heard a loud bang, ... I did not see or hear any more after that.'

Her husband (5.07.1.1) was 200 yards South of the home. He said:

'... I heard a very heavy noise of a low flying aircraft ... did not see the aeroplane, but from the sound, it was going in the direction of the Keeragh Islands ... '

Conclusions:

An accurate track reconstruction over Fethard is difficult to obtain. However, it seems probable that a Viscount arrived from Campile, Dunbrody Abbey over Saltmills, slight turn right for heading to Baginbun Head, then it carried out a steep turn right towards Slade, after which heading North and again turn right and fly over Fethard, slightly South of Grange, heading to the Keeragh Islands, when after one minute, something happened which made a big sound. The altitude did not vary too much, presumably around 1,000 feet. Several witnesses were definitely persuaded that it was a Viscount.

5.4.2.1.1.1.7 From Fethard Area to Tuskar Rock

This part of the trajectory is over the sea, so no witness reported seeing the plane, with the exception of a Spanish sailor on a German ship, who saw what is now believed to be the Viscount at the exact moment of the crash.

This Spanish sailor (7.09.1.2) was steward on board of the MS *Metric*. He said:

'I thought I saw a plane at an altitude of some three metres falling. It was more or less like a flash … on impact some water was thrown up into the air, but in a moment the sea was normal.'

A 17 years old boy (7.08.1.1), living at Bing, stated:

'I heard a noise like water running from a big pile of stones at the beach on a bad day. I looked out to the sea and I saw a column of water on the left side of the Tuskar, about at the spot where the Irish Lights ship anchors … I did not see anything going into the water … '

Both points are consistent with the location of the main wreckage.

Prior to the crash, an event may have been observed from the shore: indeed witness 7.06.1.NA. stated:

Standing at the point called 'the bar', near to Tacumshane Lake,

'… I was looking at the waves breaking over Black Rock. After some time I looked to my left; at a point between Black Rock and Carnsore Point, I saw what appeared to be a mushroom of water out to sea. I would estimate it to be about nine miles out. This position could be consistent with a track from Keeragh Island to Tuskar.'

15 other persons living in the area between Greenore point and Carnsore Point heard a heavy noise.

However all of them may not refer to the same event. In particular, some of these 15 seemed having heard the noise a few minutes before the others.

After the crash, from 1.30 pm to 3.30 pm, a metallic object was observed by 4 witnesses, from 2 different places: Newtown and Slade. This object drifted during this time from a point located 4 to 5 nautical miles East of Fethard to a point West-South-West of the Great Saltee for 2 or 3 nautical miles.

Conclusions :

The track reconstruction, between Fethard and Tuskar cannot be precise, since the aircraft flew over the sea. However, it is probable that a part separated from the aircraft when it was flying 4 to 5 nautical miles East of Fethard: this was heard, and the separated part was observed.

It is possible that some other part separated between Black Rock and Carnsore Point; but this is not cross-checked visually.

It is certain that two witnesses saw the final impact point, since their statement is consistent with the location of the main wreckage.

The statements given by the witnesses allow for technically logic assumptions explaining the degradation process of the aircraft; the duration of this degradation process is similar to this of the other accidents of the same similarity family, around 30 mn.

But two messages transcripted from the Shannon radio-comms cannot fit with this scenario.

10.51.48	712:	– Level at 170
	Shannon:	– Roger, report at Bannow
10.57.07	712	– 712, By Bannow, level 170, estimating Strumble at 03
	Shannon:	– Roger, say again time By Bannow. I got the Strumble estimate OK
	712:	– 57
	Shannon:	– OK, time 56 and a half. Change to London AWYS 131.2. Good Bye.
	712 :	– 131.2.

The information contained in these messages is entirely incompatible with the track reconstructed here-above, which shows that, at that time, the aircraft was at lower altitude, somewhere between Old Parish and the Kennedy Arboretum.

PART C

SHANNON RADIO TRANSCRIPT — CRITICAL ANALYSIS

In this section Exp'Air examine the text of the transcripts to see if there are any inconsistencies or aberrations in the continuity. It is not possible to reconcile the reconstructed track with two signals transmitted at 10.51 and 10.57 hours.

5.4.4.1 Aim of this Critical Analysis

Despite the apparent similarities between both situations, at this step of the present study and at the end of the 1970 investigation, they are fundamentally quite different.

Indeed, in 1970, the inconsistency between the estimated position of the Viscount at 1058 hours GMT and the observations made around noon (local time) by the witnesses located in Fethard drove the Investigation Commission to envisage a possible mid-air collision: this collision had a direct impact on the accident process. Now it is clear that the inconsistency between the last two messages of the Shannon R/T transcript and the positions of the Viscount as observed by the witnesses has no impact on the accident process: these two messages do not influence the initial event, the degradation process of the aircraft, the crash, and they do not influence the reaction time of the ATS for launching the Search and Rescue actions, since everything was adequately made by London ATC.

So the scenario 'as per witnesses/disabled flight' cannot be a source of imaginative speculations: it is the only answer of the International Team to their task 'to shed further light on the Tuskar Rock accident'.

Consequently the Shannon R/T transcript critical analysis is aimed simply at reducing the inconsistency which still exists inside this unique answer.

It does not present any interest for the Intern'l Team to identify who is at the origin of this possibly incorrect transcript; the Team is not skilled for that.

What is of interest is to assess on the probability of occurrence of such an irregular transcript, which misled the 1968 Investigation Commission when they based the track reconstruction on the R/T transcript.

This assessment is to be conducted keeping in mind that the Shannon ATC is a governmental service, with strict operating procedures and highly motivated civil servants (as observed during the interviews which were conducted by the Intern'l Team).

The subject matter of assessment will never be the actors themselves, but the procedures, as they appear through the data remaining available and the interviews of the still-alive witnesses.

5.4.4.2 Data available [GMT]

The data available is:

a) *Cork*
   — the transcript of the messages between Cork (TWR and APP) and 712, from 10.26 to 11.21
   — the progress strips at Cork ATC
   — a summary of interviews made at Cork on April 3 by the Aer Lingus Internal Investigation Commission

b) *Shannon*
   — the transcript of the messages between Shannon ATC and 712, from 10.39 to 10.58 and an intermediate 'aide-mémoire'
   — the transcript of the Shannon London telephone line, from 10.36 to 10.44
   — the cover letter of the Chief ATC Officer, dated 25.3.68 (addressee not identified) together with
   — the watch supervisor's report and log of action, on duty from 11.00 Z on the 24th March).
   — the reports of the ATC officers on duty this March 24, 1968
   — the progress strips at Shannon ATC.

c) *London*
   — a copy of the original tape, recording the last 2 messages of EI-AOM

— the transcript of the messages between London ATC and EI 712, EI 362, BOA 507 … from 10.53 to 11.09
— the Aircraft Accident Report for use by ATCOs
— log extracts from 11.00 to 20.40 on 24th March
— cover letter from the Chief controller to the Centre Superintendant LATC and two reports from D and Radar Controller
— report from Duty Controller at Sopley Radar.

5.4.4.3 Witnesses' Statements

Since the Senior Officer Head of Shannon ATC (1968), the Shannon Supervisor on duty till 11.00 Z and the relief Controller taking on at 10.55, are all deceased, the witnesses who were interviewed were:

The Shannon Supervisor, who was on duty from 11.00 (GMT) till the end of the afternoon; and the Controller on duty in the morning, up to 10.55 (GMT).

a) Supervisor's statements:
— The watch Supervisor assumed duty from his predecessor at 11.00 Z. When taking over, he got the information that EI-AOM Departed Cork Airport at 10.32 Z, estimating London Airport at 11.48 Z. Reported Bannow at 10.57 Z, FL 170, Estimating Strumble 11.03 Z.
— at 11.10 Z, London ATC advised Shannon ATC: no radio contact with EI-AOM.
— at 11.13 Z, London Supervisor advised Shannon Supervisor: no radio contact with EI-AOM; London had asked EI 362, flying from Dublin to Bristol, to search for West of Strumble. When he heard that, the witness thought that London had been too fast, because London did not report on the last messages they got from EI-AOM. At this time, he did not realise of the seriousness of the situation.
— at 11.18 Z, he instructed Shannon to call EI-AOM on all frequencies and facilities.
— at 11.25 Z, he informed Cork ATC 'full alert' on flight.

— at 11.35 Z, London advised that they 'are scrambling two Shackletons and one helicopter'.
— at 11.36 Z, Senior ATC Officer home advised.
— around 12.15 Z, Senior ATC Officer arrived.
— the Supervisor remained in the OPS room till 18.30 Z, with an exception of 50 mn for lunch around 13.30 Z. So he could not listen to the original R/T comms recording during this afternoon, nor the day after.

He now presumes that he could have read the transcript in 1970, at the request of the Investigation Commission. He then did not notice anything abnormal in the transcript.

During the afternoon, possibly soon in the afternoon, the Controller on duty from 10.55 Z reported to him that he did not recall exactly if the Viscount had acknowledged his instruction to switch on London AWYS.

He considered that as a request to go and listen to the play-back. He authorised the Controller to go to the play-back room, together with a technician to listen to the recording.

From his point of view, it is not possible to envisage that a team including a technician may change anything to the recording, either by an addition or by a subtraction.

He thinks that the Controller, even if remaining some time alone in the play-back room, should not have the technical capacity to make any change. In addition the procedures were very strict.

The involvement of the Senior ATC officer cannot be considered, since his personal characteristics (he was educated in the Air Corps) and since the enormous risk this should imply in front of his subordinate.

From the witness's point of view, duplication of a tape record can be made in Shannon premises, but not any change on the original record.

b) Controller's statements:

The witness was on duty, at the desk, from 8.30 Z to 10.55 Z. He then went out for lunch. He came back 50 to 60 mn later, for another period at the desk. He left the OPS room around 15.15 Z.

When at the desk, he controlled EI-AOM from 10.39 Z (his first contact with Shannon) to 10.55 Z.

Since he knew personally the 1st officer of EI-AOM, Mr Heffernan, he is of the opinion that the Capt'n was operating the R/T.

10.39:45 Z: 'By Youghal' — The witness considers it was a clear message.

10.40:00 Z: Acknowledgment of the direct routing to Strumble: unreadable; but the repetition was clear (his opinion is that the Capt'n, at the first answer, had his microphone too far from his mouth).

10.41:00 Z: 'Passing FL 90' — Clear

10.51:48 Z: 'level at 170' — slightly weak, but readable

At 10.55 Z, the witness left the OPS room.

After the witness left the OPS room at 15.15 Z, he went into the special room where the play-back equipment was installed; that room was locked; the equipment also. No one had the right to enter alone into the room. The junior officers were not authorised to penetrate, even for maintenance purpose. Usually, when a controller had, for professional purpose, to listen to a play-back record, he was accompanied by either another controller, or a supervisor, or a technician (detached from the Post Office Service).

In the present case, the witness does not remember who was accompanying him when he heard the original tape.

He heard the tape between 15.30 and 16.00 Z. He focused his attention on that part of the record corresponding to his time on duty, but he heard the complete tape. He does not remember anything abnormal.

He did not know how long a single tape could record: in his opinion, it was 24 hours. And the change of the tape could take place near to noon, or very soon in the afternoon. He does not remember when exactly the tape was replaced on that Sunday.

There was another tape for the recording of the phone

conversations with London, presumably with the same characteristics.

According to the rule, he did not contribute in the generation of the transcript. He read it only two years later, when the accident report was published and the annex related to the radio-comms forwarded to ATC Shannon.

At that time, he observed that there were two errors in the report: Shannon (and not Cork) gave the authorisation 'Direct to Strumble', and the Viscount acknowledged (when it was stated in the report that it did not). These remarks were not transmitted to the Head of the Investigation Team since they were considered by the Senior ATC Officer of minor importance.

Summary of the ATC witnesses' statements
From their recalls, they did not notice anything abnormal in the execution of the procedures on that day, neither by themselves, nor by their fellows on duty. None of them contributed, in accordance with the procedures, to the writing of the transcript of the radio-comms; when they reread it, they did not identify anything abnormal.

c) These statements of ATC members may be usefully complemented by those of one of the major responsible members of the 1968 Investigation Commission, who stated that:
   — The estimated position at 58 was derived from the messages read on the Shannon R/T transcript.
   — The Investigation Commission was concerned for long by a '1 and a half minutes early at Bannow ... but taking into account the accurate position was indeterminate since the transfer to ATC London depended on the traffic at any particular moment'.
   — Since the estimated position at 1058, **all statements provided by witnesses located West of Waterford were ignored,** and considered not relevant to the Viscount but to the Search airplanes in the afternoon.

— He listened by himself to the tape recording of the Shannon R/T on the Wednesday or Thursday following the Sunday of the accident. He listened to that tape at the occasion of a visit that the Commission paid to Shannon ATC.

'The tape I heard was readable because I had a copy of the transcript made by ATC experts. The footnote *"RT transmissions from EI 712 were generally very poor"* referred to is put on every transcript I ever saw. It is the same as *Errors and omissions excepted*.'

— The Institute of Research and Standards made a loop to determine the altitude (5,000 or 12,000 feet). They made a copy of this loop (connecting the first minutes of the London AWYS comms recording to the last few minutes of the Shannon tape). This was sent to the USA (for further acoustic research).

— The tape(s) on which were recorded the Shannon ATC R/T with EI-AOM have been re-used by the ATC around the years 1976, after the authorisation had been given to the ATC by Dublin ATS.

5.4.4.4 Analysis

The period of time to be analysed for a better appreciation of the 1968 Shannon ATC procedures, spread from 10.32 Z, take-off time, to 11.25 Z 'Full alert on Flight'.

The first step in the analysis is to comment on the Shannon R/T transcript and the Shannon–London telephone line transcript.

5.4.4.4.1 R/T Transcript (all Z times)

The R/T on Shannon frequency was preceded by the last communications with Cork.

At 10.38 (Cork time):
EI 712:   712, out of FL70
Cork: Roger, 712 cleared on course. Change to Shannon 127.5
EI 712:   Cheerio

Comment: the average climb rate from take-off is 1,150 feet/mn

At 10.39:45 (Shannon time):

EI 712:	Good morning
Shannon:	Good morning
EI 712:	By Youghal, passing through 75, climbing to 170, Tuskar 57

Comments:
1. According to the SATCO (refer Appendix 5.4h), following a question asked in the course of the Investigation (October 13, 1969), the exact time on the recorder was 54 sec later. Consequently 10.39:45 should read 10.40:39 (comment valid for the whole transcript).
2. Between 10.38.00 (Cork time) and 10.39:45 (Shannon time) which means either 1mn, 45 sec or 2 mn 39 sec (exact time at Shannon), the Viscount climbed 500 feet.

A discontinuity appears in the climb rate, which shows a 'timing' problem.

At 10.40:00

Shannon:	712, if you wish, you may route direct to Strumble.
EI 712:	(unreadable)
Shannon:	Your transmission is fairly unreadable here. Confirm you are accepting a direct routing to Strumble.
EI 712:	Affirmative, estimating Strumble at 03.
Shannon:	Roger, call cruising.

Comments:
1. Everything said after the proposal 'you may route direct to Strumble' **is not transcripted** in an *aide-mémoire* which was presumably used by the Investigation Commission **since this document is in their files.**
2. It is possible that the error which is introduced in the accident report, stating that there was no acknowledgment by

EI 712, is in relation to the existence of this *aide-mémoire*. However, the certified transcript is dated 25 March 1968 (the day after the crash).

3. The ATC on duty considers that the 'unreadable' answer of EI 712 could be due to a wrong position of the microphone near the mouth of the Captain. According to the same, what was said just before and just after was clear.

4. The estimate Strumble at 03 comes after an unreadable message and a message giving the estimate to Tuskar at 57. An estimate direct Strumble at 03 is approximately 4 mn sooner than the estimate via Tuskar, when it should not be, in the usual conditions, sooner than 1 mn.

A discontinuity appears in the estimates, between 10.39:45 and 10.40.

At 10.41:20:

Shannon: Your present level?

EI 712: Passing 90

Shannon: Arrange your climb to cross the boundary at 170

EI 712: unreadable

— The transcript, then, shows messages with GAPMC and EI 112.

EI 112 leaves Shannon frequency at 10.43:15.

GAPMC leaves Shannon frequency at 10.47.

— From 10.47: EI 712 is the only flight controlled by Shannon.

Comments:

1. Shannon asks for the present flight level of EI 712 at 10.41:20, 1 mn 30 sec after having been informed that EI 712 was crossing FL 75, climbing.

Shannon does not include the flight identification in his call, when 2 other flights were listening on his frequency.

It may be questioned how, 1 mn after the last exchange, EI 712 knew that the question was to him, if he was not the only flight under Shannon control.

2. Between 10.39.^{45} and 10.41.^{20}, EI 712 climbed 1,500 feet; the average climb rate is 1,000 feet/mn.
3. The second unreadable message is not followed, as for the first one, by a request of acknowledgment.
4. Two messages being considered 'clear' by the controller are preceded and followed by two 'unreadable messages'. No further unreadable messages were transcripted.

At 10.51:48:

EI 712:   Level at 170
Shannon: Report at Bannow

Comments:

1. The origin of the call from EI 712 is not identified, but at that time EI 712 was the only flight controlled by Shannon. In addition, the controller stated that he could identify the voice of the Captain, since the transmission was good.
2. The average climb rates are as follows:
    from 0 to FL 170: 850 feet /mn
    from FL 90 to FL 170: 760 feet/mn.
    — The Controller on duty changed at 10.55 .

At 10.57:07:

EI 712:   712, by Bannow, level 170, estimating Strumble at 03.
Shannon: Say again the time 'by Bannow'. I got the Strumble estimate OK.
EI 712:   57.
Shannon: OK. Time 56 and a half; change now to London Airways 131.2
EI 712:   131.2.

Comments:

1. The Controller on duty reacts to the time observed when passing 'by Bannow' whereas he does not react to the estimate Strumble at 03.

Between the theoretical position of 'by Bannow' and Strumble, the distance is 44 nautical miles; an estimate Strumble at 11.03 implies a ground speed by 440 kts, which is, by far, impossible.

But the Controller reacts to an inaccuracy of 30 sec on a past event!

It is to be observed that the estimate Strumble was of major importance for London ATC, who had in charge to manage at the best the introduction of the EI 712 flight in the Heathrow traffic.

2. The correction made by the Controller on duty with respect to the timing at 'by Bannow' is considered by the still alive witnesses in line with his psychological characteristics.

Taking these characteristics into account, the estimate Strumble confirms the discontinuity observed at 10.40.00.

3. The exact time on the recorder when the ATCO said 56 and a half was 10.57 and a half (refer document in Appendix 5.4h).

— The transcript stops at 10.57:29; this prevents of any analysis of what was radioed later on that frequency. Was there any garbled, or unreadable EI 712 emission around 10.58? When were emitted further calls to EI 712?

5.4.4.4.2 Shannon–London Telephone Line Transcript (all Z times)

At 10.36:
Shannon: 712 is FL 170 and it is Strumble at 11.07
London: OK

Comments:
The estimate Strumble at 07 is consistent with the flight plan filed up by the co-pilot.

At 10.38:20:
Shannon: Have you any objections to the Irish 712 routing direct from Cork to Strumble?

10.39:
London: None at all.

Comments:
This request to London is made just before EI 712 switches on Shannon frequency, at 10.39:45.

Acceptance from London cleared direct routing proposed to EI 712 at 10.40.

Between 10.39 and 10.43:00:
Exchange of information on Flight Speedbird 501
At 10.43:00:
Shannon: A revision on Aer Lingus 712. It is estimating Strumble at 11.03 and is routing Cork direct to Strumble ...
London: OK

Exchange of information on flight EI 362
10.44:
Shannon: Aer Lingus 712 is routing direct to Strumble. Is that OK?
London: Yes that's all right.

Comments:
— **An estimate direct Strumble at 03 should be consistent with a take-off Cork at 10.27 [Author's note: EI-AOM took off at 10.32].**
— The Shannon transcript (telephone line) stops at 10.44; this prevents of any analysis of what has been exchanged between Shannon and London controllers on duty, which could allow to cross-check the various logs of actions and reports made by each of the concerned personnel.
— This is of interest in particular for the period just after minute 58, when the London Controller informed and questioned his Shannon partner about the distress message.
— The London transcript has been requested from the London ATC through the AAIB; but the quest was unsuccessful.

5.4.4.4.3 Assessment

A valuable assessment should need some complementary information which is not available at the present day. The unavailability of the original tapes is of importance.

The duration of the two Shannon radio and telephone transmission transcripts should have covered up to 11.25, when the 'full alert' was declared.

A valuable information could refer to the conditions under which were executed the previous EI 712 flights between Cork and Heathrow.

5.4.4.6 Conclusion of the Critical Analysis of the Shannon R/T Transcript

* Since there are on one hand about 50 independent witnesses,
* since each of their statements is consistent with the other ones, and allows for a complete track reconstruction and for a technically logical description of the degradation process of EI-AOM,
* since there is on the other side, the transcript of two messages which were exchanged on the Shannon ATC frequency during a period of time when EI-AOM was the only flight under their control,
* since several questions are still pending, and cannot be answered, unfortunately, **the opinion of the Intern'l Team is that the weak side of the inconsistency is that of Shannon ATC.** But this opinion cannot be evidenced.

This opinion gives some light on the reasons why the 1968 Investigation Commission could not conclude their accident report.

Neither this opinion, nor the final truth, if it can be obtained at a time, has a direct impact on the accident process, from the initial event to the Search and Rescue activities.

Appendix 4

THE FINAL CONCLUSIONS OF THE 2002 INTERNATIONAL STUDY TEAM PRESENTED IN DUBLIN ON 24 JANUARY 2002

6. CONCLUSIONS OF THE STUDY

The International Team (IT) reached the following conclusions:

6.0: Historical background

6.0.1 The formal accident report (AAP) N° 6 issued on 30 June 1970 was deficient in that insufficient effort was made to thoroughly reconstruct the track of the aircraft and that pertinent material was excluded.

6.0.2 The Review Report issued in June 2000 is a thorough, impartial and professional review of files pertaining to the accident. It clarified many issues and uncovered significant new material.

6.0.3 The data still available today, on which to base a study, are as follows:

— All requested accident reports from other Viscount accidents obtained from the respective national AIUs.
— Partial files of AOM accident investigation
— Partial technical data of the Viscount aircraft.
— Partial operational data of the Viscount.

No Aer Lingus maintenance record and no material part of EI-AOM were provided for examination but several witnesses' statements, either delivered in 1968 or later, were available.

Consequently, the present study cannot lead to the issuance of an ICAO type accident report. In accordance with the mission letter, this study is aimed at shedding further light on the circumstances surrounding the accident to Aer Lingus Vickers Viscount 803 EI-AOM.

6.1: With respect to the presence of another air mobile:

6.1.1 The 1970 accident report AAP N° 6 was inconclusive, and although no cause was found, the suggestion was made in the report that the presence of another aircraft in the area was inescapable. As a consequence, several 'Theories' attempted to provide consistent answers, such as:

— Collision or near collision with a missile,
— Collision or near collision with a drone,
— Collision with a manned aircraft.

And some others, including 'conspiracy' theories, which are still alive …

6.1.2 An analysis based on the technical and operational characteristics of the British missiles and drones operated in 1968, shows a collision between such air mobiles launched from the UK ranges or ships and the Irish Viscount, in the vicinity of Tuskar Rock, was technically possible but it is impossible that, after the collision, this un-manned aircraft be seen over Fethard, in the conditions reported by the witnesses.

The analysis of the scenario based on a collision with a manned aircraft shows that, although such a scenario is operationally possible, it does not fit in with the statements of witnesses. And there is no aircraft which could have crashed on that day.

The scenario based on the assumption that AOM never recovered from its initial loss of control ignores the statements of all the witnesses and is lacking substantiation.

The International Team have carefully examined all aspects of the tests conducted in the UK ranges and of the sea and air activities performed on that Sunday. It is their opinion that all theories involving the presence of another aircraft can be rejected.

6.2: With respect to the Flight reconstruction:

6.2.1 All ways explored being 'dead ends', the only one remaining was to question the basis on which the 1968 investigation was built. This basis, used for the AOM Flight reconstruction, was the radio-comms transcript of Shannon ATC.

6.2.2 Following the statements of the witnesses, who answered the 'call for witnesses' emitted at the end of the year 2000, and taking into account the statements received in 1968, which were discounted at the time, since they could not fit with the flight construction based on the R/T transcripts, it was possible to reconstruct the following EI-AOM accident process.

— First loss of control over Old Parish between 11.42 and 11.44 local time. (GMT 10.42 and 10.44)
— Disabled flight from Old Parish to Tramore Bay, Brownstown Head, Tory Hill and Kennedy Arboretum
— Second loss of control over Kennedy Arboretum at 11.58, and emission of the distress message on London Airways control frequency
— Disabled flight around Slievecoiltra Hill, over Ballykelly, Fethard, Saltees Islands, the Barrels
— Crash at Tuskar Rock at approximately 12.15.

The aircraft degradation process lasted for around 30 minutes and included the separation of an object, possibly the port elevator or part of it, East of Fethard, and probably the separation of the port tailplane over the Barrels.

It is to be noted that the above description is based on the statements of 46 witnesses, 24 of them being eye-witnesses, and 8 of them having identified a green and silver coloured Viscount. The statements given in March/April 1968 were laid with the Gardaí.

As a consequence of the number of eye-witnesses, the opinion of the International Team is that the Flight track reconstruction is essentially as described in § 6.2.2, and not as described in the 1970 accident report.

6.2.3 The content of the last two messages radioed on the ATC Shannon frequency reporting 'level at FL 170' and 'By

Bannow, flight level 170', cannot fit with that flight reconstruction.

6.2.4 A possible assumption has been to consider that the crew irregularly reported the aircraft position in each of these two messages. However, a detailed assessment drives to the conclusion that this deviation out of the IFR flight plan is an hypothesis which is extremely unlikely.

6.2.5 Consequently, the inconsistency between the track reconstruction and the R/T Shannon transcript can be solved only if it is possible to identify the cause of an error in the transcript of the R/T communications issued by Shannon ATC.

The data available today, and the interviews of the two still alive witnesses do not allow for such an identification.

However, some observations may be significant:

— The original tapes are not available: either they have been lost when the holder Service moved, or they have been re-used by Shannon ATC (in the seventies) with the authorisation of hierarchical Authorities.

— The extracts of the tapes, transcripted as relevant by Shannon ATC do not cover the complete period to be analysed.

— There are no exhaustive detailed chronological reports of the controllers and of the supervisor acting at the time of the accident.

— A detailed analysis of the contents of the messages indicates some discontinuities in the flight parameters, or some atypical reactions either from the acting Controller, or from the Captain (e.g. ETA Strumble).

Consequently, the opinion of the International Team is that the procedures which were applied in ATC Shannon at the time of the accident were either not well adapted (in particular for specific period of a transition between routine and emergency), or not carefully applied.

6.2.6 However, it is of importance to note that a dysfunction in Shannon ATC, if any occurred, did not have any detrimental consequence on the cause of the accident, nor on the degradation process of the Viscount.

6.3: With respect to the cause of the accident:

6.3.1 The method for identifying the probable cause of the AOM accident could not be based on the observation of the material parts of the wreckage, which were not available.

As a consequence, the International Team took advantage of the lessons learned from events in the whole life of the Viscount and certain other aircraft types, and compared to the AOM accident, those accidents which showed a similar loss of control, followed by some period of disabled flight.

6.3.2 This comparison concludes that the initial events causing a degradation process of the aircraft similar to the one suffered by EI-AOM could be :
— Door strike
— Bird strike
— Spigot rupture in the spring tab mechanism
— Structure failure
— Severe recovering manoeuvres, alone, or in conjunction one with the other(s).

6.3.3 The technical investigation carried out as part of the initial investigation and presented as appendix material to the 1970 report was thorough and shows the enormous amount of dedicated work which went into the search, salvage and engineering investigation of the accident. Nevertheless it must be noted that with the exception of the fin, portion of the rudder and portions of two elevator tabs, nothing was recovered aft of the rear pressure bulkhead. The tailplanes, elevators and fuselage structure in the tailcone area were all missing.

6.3.4 Since the Investigation Commission accepted the position of the manufacturers which was not to open discussion on the matters related to the non-recovered parts, no conclusions on what could have happened to the empennage were established.

6.3.5 No maintenance documentation specific to the actual aircraft, was made available to the International Team.

There is no reason that the International Team contest the 2000 Review conclusions:

— There is no evidence to suggest that any omission or error in the Inspection Visit 2.04 of the previous 1967 December contributed in any way to the accident.
— But serious errors in Aer Lingus maintenance scheduling may be indicative of a less than ideal work culture existing in the airline at that time.

6.3.6 The present technical analysis, which accepted that there was impairment of the pitch control and lack of lateral stability of the aircraft, resulted in the identification of the need to consider as possible causal factors, the following events:

— Door strike
— Bird strike
— Metal corrosion
— Maintenance error
— Metal fatigue
— Flutter which could have damaged or affected the following components:
— Tailplane
— Elevator, including tabs
— Systems: pitch control

6.3.7 Operational considerations made possible to 'narrow the field' of the possible assumptions.

A door strike or a failure of the main structure of the aircraft could be discounted as an initial triggering factor of the EI-AOM upset.

A review of the aircraft in-service experience, and, in particular, a number of defects and accidents which occurred posterior to that of EI-AOM, lead to the International Team's opinion as follows:

— **An initial event, which cannot be clearly identified, is considered to be some form of distress affecting the horizontal tail of the aircraft. Possible causal factors are metal fatigue, corrosion, flutter or a bird strike.**
— **It is possible that the sensitivity to negative accelerations of the engine fuel control unit and oil pressure supply to torque meter system were contributory factors.**

— The recovering manoeuvres of the aircraft following the initial upset and the subsequent flight would have been outside the airworthiness certification envelope and may have resulted in some deformation of the structure.
— A progressive failure of the structure of the port tail plane and elevator is consistent with the observations relating to the ultimate attitudes of the aircraft.

Excessive spring tab free play resulting in the fatigue failure of a component in the tab operating mechanism could have induced a tailplane-elevator tab free flutter condition.

The consequence of a 6hz tab free induced elevator/ tailplane flutter, according to the manufacturer, would be the generation of large elevator and tailplane forces capable of exciting the fuselage, thus producing severe vibrations.

The loads induced in the tailplane would be sufficient to cause a structural fatigue failure within the timescale observed for EI-AOM.

6.3.8 There was no involvement of any other aircraft or missile.

6.4: With respect to the crew behaviour:

6.4.1 Several witnesses' statements support the opinion that the Viscount EI-AOM left the track planned in the Flight Plan.

6.4.2 From the available data, it may be concluded that this deviation from the Flight Plan was most unlikely to have been due to a deliberate decision of the Captain.

6.4.3 The observed aircraft attitudes, with sudden and rough variations of the flight and engines parameters led to the opinion that the impairment of the stability of the aircraft was the cause of such exceptional movements for a transport aircraft.

6.4.4 The crew had to face a situation when, after the first upset, the aircraft was out of its certification envelope.

Extremely high control forces, possibly reaching as high as 450 pounds, had to be manually countered. The crew probably used the pitching effect of the engine power to stabilise the aircraft in pitch.

The tail, probably asymmetric from suffering damage may have affected the stability of the Viscount.

The very poor manoeuvrability of the Viscount during the degradation process explains why the crew could not come back to Cork, nor land or ditch on the large strands they know along the coast.

It is the International Team's opinion that it was a major achievement for the crew to be able to keep this aircraft flying for more than half an hour, with such poor manoeuvrability characteristics. This showed a remarkable intrinsic and professional level of experience. It is equitable to acknowledge such a performance.

6.5: Final comments:

6.5.1 It is the International Team's opinion that the track reconstruction can be considered of factual nature, since it is substantiated by the consistent statements of so many witnesses, whilst the cause and the causal factors of the initial event and the description of the degradation process of the aircraft are of conjectural nature, since there is no longer available any piece of evidence.

6.5.2 The quest of further objective technical data appears to be a lengthy (and possibly unsuccessful) process, and, very costly in the present conditions. For information, an estimate from BAE to the very first Request For Quotation is given in Appendix 6.a.

6.5.3 The Maintenance Files are no longer available in the Aer Lingus or in the Irish CAA archives.

6.5.4 The last 25 mn flight of AOM and AOF aircraft show noticeable similarities.

A further examination of the EI-AOF accident files may be of interest.

As a conclusion, the International Team is of the opinion that the files of the EI-AOM accident should be closed.

REQUEST FROM THE AUTHOR

I am anxious to contact certain persons. This request applies in particular to farmers and fishermen in the south-east region of Ireland. If any unfamiliar piece of metal, especially of aluminium or its alloys, was discovered on land since 1968, and still exists, the author is very interested in it.

The same request applies to any fisherman who may have trawled such an object in the seas near the Saltee Islands, The Barrels, Coningmore Half Tide Rock, Carnsore Point, Greenore Point, Tuskar Rock, or northwards to positions abeam of Cahore Point and the Blackwater region. The item may have appeared nondescript, perhaps covered in marine growth or small crustaceans.

I would also welcome contact from any person who may have photographed a silver-coloured object which remained afloat on the day of the crash. It was observed awash by witnesses for three hours, floating between Fethard and a point west-south-west of Great Saltee Island. It is irrelevant if the quality of the print is poor, or if the object seems too far away. Modern computer enhancement can work miracles.

I can be contacted at the simple mail address of Ashford, Co. Wicklow. I can arrange collection of any item, and any photo will be returned.

Index